*The Love of*
*Italian Cooking*

The Love of

# Italian Cooking

Mary Reynolds   Foreword by Armando Orsini

octopus

# FOREWORD
## by Armando Orsini

One of the most fascinating things about Italy is that it is a land of great contrasts; the old and modern sometimes clash but many times blend in a lovely harmony and even when they don't, we must recognize the worth and beauty of one or the other taken by itself. To sit on a 16th century Florentine armchair can be pure aesthetic joy, but then to lounge on a very modern armchair designed and sleekly made in Milano can give the same sense of elegance and comfort. Similarly we have the great mountains – the Alps, contrasting the flattest plains of the Po Valley; the Roman Colosseum and the ultra modern sky-scrapers in Milano.

The same drama is a part of the Italian 'cuisine' or as I prefer *la cucina Italiana*. The 'Love of Italian Cooking' has correlated this rich past and the present. Mary Reynolds has researched and collected a variety of recipes from the very classic *Zuppa di Pesce* (page 73), as old as Venice itself, to the 18th century *Timballo di Riso con Scampi* (page 74), a dish prepared at great houses in fancy moulds and served in different shapes. And the author has not neglected to include more modern recipes such as *Anitra Arrosto al Marsala* (page 83), modern because Marsala wine was introduced after 1861.

From the elaborate Roman feasts through the sombre Middle Ages to the opulence of the Renaissance and the sophistication of modern times, *la cucina Italiana* has given inspiration and delight to other countries. There is even an underground story that a small dark Italian went to China long before Marco Polo and taught the Chinese how to make the famous egg noodles. In the past Caterina de Medici brought our *cucina* to the Court of France and developed the French modern *haute cuisine*. Now there is no great Lady from Florence but a new breed of restaurateurs, like myself, who have introduced the joy of Italian food around the world.

It is amazing how events coincide, like scientists in different countries simultaneously discovering a cure or a new bacteria. Similarly coincidental, in the sixties, hundreds of Italian restaurants were opened in different parts of the world. One of the tasks of their owners has been to 'educate' patrons to the taste of real Italian food. I say 'educate' because people in Europe and to a greater extent in the U.S.A. had the wrong idea about our *cucina* for many years, believing spaghetti and meat balls or pizza to be the ultimate in Italian food!

These restaurants in London, Madrid, Berlin, Stockholm, Paris, New York, Beverly Hills and so forth, have encouraged people to truly and sensitively appreciate our kind of cooking. Many want to know how to prepare it themselves and learn about the ingredients, including the herbs. Basil, for example, the staple herb for many of the freshest sauces, is found in many gardens; in winter it is grown indoors – often on window-sills of city apartments, yet for years basil was almost unknown.

With this curiosity to know more about our food this excellent book has much to offer. Recipes are presented regionally, which particularly suits the colourful Italian history. Until 1861 Italy was a collection of individual principalities and their own distinguished tastes in food are still very much persistant. Furthermore it is fun to prepare a whole meal from a particular area. What a marvellous idea for a hostess who has prepared a lunch or dinner to say to her guests, 'Now we will dine as in Tuscany', and of course the wine served will be a young Chianti or an older and more robust Riserva Ducale Ruffino. There is always the additional pleasure of being reminded of one's travel; preparing the *Peperonata* eaten in Milano, the *Gnocchi Verdi* sampled in Florence or the *Risotto Veronese* tasted in Verona at the 12 Apostoli Restaurant.

I myself have found inspiring new dishes in this book and look forward to trying them in the kitchen of my New York restaurant; I expect they will find their place on my menu.

A book like this can stay on your kitchen shelf for at least twenty years and still, after that, you will find the recipes valid; after all I know of one recipe in this book, *Pollo al Mattone* (page 50), that has lasted 2000 years.

First published 1978 by
Octopus Books Limited
59 Grosvenor Street
London W1

© 1978 Octopus Books Limited

ISBN 0 7064 0694 X

Produced by Mandarin Publishers Limited
22a Westlands Road
Quarry Bay, Hong Kong

Printed in Hong Kong

# CONTENTS

# Introduction

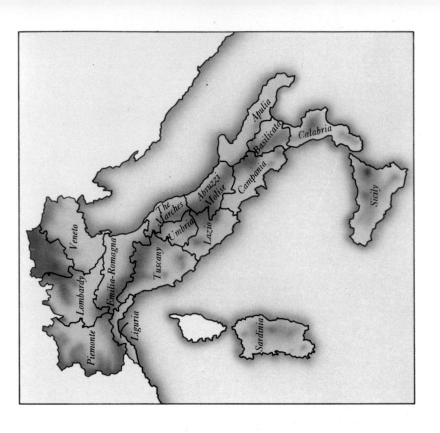

Love is an essential ingredient in Italian cooking. For mamma is the dominant influence in the Italian kitchen, lovingly planning, shopping for, preparing and cooking the dishes that become the focal point of that noisy, convivial occasion, the main meal, when all the family gathers round the table to exchange gossip and discuss the events of the day while enjoying mamma's cooking.

What is the secret that years later makes Italians in every part of the world speak yearningly of home cooking? It begins with shopping. The traditional Italian mamma doesn't just shop, she goes to the market and *selects*, examining, comparing and finally choosing the best of whatever is in season and therefore good value; the shiniest peppers, the plumpest chicken, the tiniest squid, the youngest and sweetest peas. She chooses in the knowledge that each and every ingredient matters, because even when combined with other foods the individual ingredients contribute their own colour, flavour and texture rather than merging into an undistinguished whole. Italian food is very much the creation of Italian housewives; simple, colourful and tasty rather than sophisticated, yet stamped with touches of originality that are mamma's own special contribution to otherwise standard recipes.

## Regional Cooking

If you imagine that the cooking is much the same all over Italy you're in for a big surprise. The cooking of the people, but not necessarily that of tourist hotels and restaurants, is intensely regional. A quick look at the history of the country will remind you that until 1861 Italy was a collection of autonomous states, each with its own customs and traditions. Many of these regional characteristics are still much in evidence today, as a study of the people, their occupations, the architecture of their cities and their food, wine and cooking quickly reveals.

The difference between the prosperous industrial North and the slower, more rural and poorer Southern regions is well known. But almost any journey from one region to another reveals essential differences. Where cooking is concerned the differences spring from local produce. The cooking of Trentino, between Lombardy and Piemonte, is so influenced by bordering countries that it is not truly Italian and has been excluded.

The Italian housewife with a large family to feed, often on slender means, has always concentrated on making the best of what is available — invariably vegetables and herbs, cereals, cheese, fruit and, in coastal areas, fish, with poultry, game and meat being added as the budget permits. For instance, where the olive tree flourishes, in Liguria, Tuscany and the Southern regions, olive oil is the natural cooking medium, but in the North the milk from the dairy herds produces butter and cheese, so butter is commonly used in the kitchen.

## Eating in an Italian Home

The day begins with the usual frugal continental breakfast, *prima colazione*, of coffee and rolls. The main meal, *pranzo*, is often taken at midday but sometimes in the evenings, whichever best suits the family. It always consists of at least three courses, sometimes four or five. An average family meal begins with *minestra* which is the most characteristically Italian part of the meal. The choice of *minestra* is wide and to a large extent regional; it may be a soup or a pasta, rice or vegetable dish. Pasta and rice are invariably served as a separate course and not as an accompaniment to meat or poultry. The *minestra* is followed by a main course of meat, fish or poultry often served with a vegetable, and is followed by a salad or a single raw vegetable such as young broad (lima) beans or shredded fennel. A sweet is sometimes served after the main

6

course, but more often cheese and/or fresh fruit instead. A small cup of very strong black coffee rounds off the meal.

A light luncheon, *colazione*, or a supper, *cena*, invariably begins with a huge bowl of soup followed by an egg, cheese or vegetable dish, with fruit to finish. In warm weather soup is sometimes served *semi-freddo* (lukewarm) or cold but it is always an important part of the meal and is served in wide, deep plates so that the grated cheese can be stirred in without spilling the soup.

## Eating Out

If you want to eat as the Italians do rather than as tourists are expected to, you must forsake restaurants and hotels in the main piazzas and seek out the *trattorie* (small family-run eating houses) in side streets, especially those patronised by the people of the town. Make a habit of asking for local dishes, cheeses and wines, details of which can usually be obtained at the tourist office.

Don't be discouraged if items on the menu sound strange. Local dialect can give a familiar dish an entirely different name, a fact which often confuses Italians as much as the rest of us. Never be afraid to ask; if they've time to spare there's nothing Italians like more than discussing food! They'll tell you in the greatest detail exactly how to prepare their favourite dishes, where you can buy the best ingredients and the 'right' utensils. In Tuscany you'll learn the advantages of a *mattone* (see page 50) for cooking chicken, in Emilia-Romagna how to use a pasta machine for rolling and cutting *pasta all' uova*, in Liguria how to prepare *pesto* (see page 66), and in Campania how to judge the condition of the Mozzarella.

## Italian Wines

Italy is the world's largest wine producer. Although vast quantities are consumed in Italy increasing amounts are being exported, and you are likely to find most of the wines mentioned in the chapter introductions of this book on your local wine merchant's shelves.

Most Italian wines are made from indigenous varieties of hill grown grapes which make them easily distinguishable from the wines of other countries. Italian wines also differ markedly from each other, their individual characteristics depending on soil, climate, the variety of grape used and the method of vinification.

In 1963 Italy passed a law giving nationally enforceable protection to named wines from specific areas. It created the *Denominazione di Origine Controllata* (D.O.C.), which means that only wines genuinely produced within a legally delimited area can be sold under the name of that area. The letters D.O.C. on the label means that the wine is of 'particular reputation and worth'. There is also a simple denomination for wines of lesser worth, and a rare denomination, the D.O.C.G., for really outstanding wines.

When travelling in Italy it is usually better value to drink the wine of the region you happen to be in, and often unnamed carafe wines turn out to be excellent. It is helpful when choosing wines to remember the

following label terms: *secco* (dry), *abboccato* (medium sweet), *amabile* (sweet), *dolce* (very sweet), *amaro* (bitter or very dry), *frizzante* (semi-sparkling), *spumante* (sparkling), *vecchio* (old), *riserva* (guarantee ageing), *classico* (from the best area of its region).

As there is plenty available, local wine is a natural ingredient in regional dishes. Dryish white, and red wines are used mostly in meat and poultry dishes and fish stews. For braised or stewed meats, wine is added after the initial browning of the meat, and then allowed to bubble briskly until it has almost disappeared – part of it having evaporated and the rest permeated the meat and so helped to tenderise and flavour it. Marsala, the rich, fortified Sicilian wine, is used for flavouring sweet dishes and also, with delectable results, in chicken, veal, duck and ham recipes. A medium rather than a very sweet or dry Marsala is best for cooking, and it keeps for months even after the bottle has been opened.

Dry white vermouth is exceedingly useful in the kitchen, and again it keeps well after opening. Using a lesser amount, it can deputise for white wine in savoury recipes. Italy also has many liqueurs which have a useful role to play in the kitchen. These include Arum (orange liqueur), Strega (herb and orange flavoured) and Maraschino (cherry liqueur).

## Using this Book

The selection of regional, and mostly traditional, recipes in this book can be reproduced with reasonable faithfulness in other countries. Portion sizes have been scaled down to suit most people, but increase them if you are catering for Italian appetites, especially pasta and rice dishes, and soups. To achieve an authentic flavour and texture it is important to use the ingredients stated, or, as second best, the substitutes. Excellent as it is, grated Cheddar cheese cannot reproduce the characteristic spiciness of good, freshly grated Parmesan or Pecorino, nor can an ordinary rice produce the texture of a risotto made with top quality Italian rice. On the other hand Italian canned peeled tomatoes and tomato purée (paste) often reproduce the richness of sun ripened tomatoes better than the fresh but picked green variety available in more northerly countries.

Grow fresh herbs if you possibly can, especially oregano, basil, marjoram, mint and flat-leaved parsley, because they add a genuine Italian flavour to your cooking. Keep small quantities of spices in stock and renew them before they have a chance to become stale. And if your store cupboard contains jars of capers, cans of anchovies, tuna fish, artichoke hearts, olives plus dried mushrooms, Italian rice and a selection of pastas you will always have the basic ingredients for 'cooking Italian' whenever you feel like it.

Remember that there are no hard and fast rules where Italian recipes are concerned. Mamma adds a little of this or more of that to suit her own family or to use what happens to be available, and you should do the same. Taste, consider, and taste again, and don't forget that love and care are essential ingredients of Italian cookery.

# Sicily & Sardinia

Our gastronomic journey through the regions of Italy starts in the islands where, in a sense, much of it began. The Sicilians learned the secrets of Greek cooking from their conquerors more than 2000 years ago in much the same way as the Sardinians learned from the Phoenicians. Arabian, African, Saracen and Roman influences have since left their mark, and historically the islands have shared a common background of poverty and isolation from the mainland of Italy. But here the similarities end; the people, the countryside and the cooking of each island are quite unlike those of the other.

Sicily is mountainous, volcanic and dotted with the remains of Greek and Roman civilizations, while the Sicilians themselves are volatile, ebullient and hardy. As they live on an island, their cooking is based mainly on home produce, and this includes vast quantities of excellent vegetables, citrus and other fruits, nuts and wine. The lack of good meat is more than compensated for by the quality and variety of fish caught all around the coast. Fish is important in the Sicilian diet, and shellfish, dogfish, sardines, grey mullet, tuna and swordfish are among the species commonly enjoyed. Sicilian cooking is generally robust in flavour and colourful in appearance. Bread and pasta are important foods and olive oil is used a great deal for cooking.

Sicilians have a sweet tooth and their desserts, pastries and ices have achieved worldwide fame. The renowned *cassata*, originally a rich and decorative gâteau made to celebrate feast days, is now more widely known as a multi-flavoured ice cream dessert. Both the *cassata* and the crisp, golden pastry cylinders known as *cannoli* have delicious fillings of sweetened Ricotta cheese, flavoured with candied peel, glacé (candied) cherries, nuts, chocolate and liqueurs. A Sicilian is reputed to have brought ices to Europe, and genuine Sicilian fruit and water ices are a revelation. Wines are produced in large quantities and include Marsala, a rich fortified wine invaluable in the kitchen.

Sardinia is a much flatter and more tranquil island than Sicily, though still rugged, and the main occupations are farming and fishing. The people are more reserved than the Sicilians, and many of them still live in relative isolation tending their herds of sheep and goats. Much of the cooking is of a simple nature. Traditionally whole baby lambs, sucking pigs, young goats or game are spit-roasted over open fires of juniper and olive wood, a method of cooking known as *a furia furia*.

Sardinian wives make a special bread which is considered a symbol of family unity. Its very thin, crackling texture gives it the name *carta da musica*. Sardinia has much the same pasta dishes as the mainland, but retains its own special fish dishes and fish soups. These are not easy to reproduce as the species of fish caught are not always available in other countries. *Bottarga* (or *Buttariga*) is a unique antipasto consisting of the compressed and dried eggs of the grey mullet. Sardinian cooking more than compensates for its lack of sophistication by the glimpses it gives of simple, ancient cooking techniques, long forgotten in other parts of the world.

9

# CAPONATA

*Vegetable Antipasto*

This subtle sweet-sour combination of vegetables makes an unusual cold starter, served either on its own or with hard-boiled (hard-cooked) eggs, cold fish or chicken. The secret of a *caponata* is to cook the vegetables separately until the final simmering, so that each retains its individual identity. This dish keeps for several days in a refrigerator.

**Metric/Imperial**

0.5 kg/1¼ lb aubergines
salt
4 sticks celery
5 × 15 ml spoons/5 tablespoons olive oil
freshly ground black pepper
100 g/4 oz onion, chopped
1 × 400 g/14 oz can peeled tomatoes, drained
1 × 15 ml spoon/1 tablespoon tomato purée
2–3 × 15 ml spoons/2–3 tablespoons wine vinegar
25 g/1 oz sugar
2 × 15 ml spoons/2 tablespoons drained capers
12 small green olives, stoned
1 × 15 ml spoon/1 tablespoon pine nuts

**American**

1¼ lb eggplants
salt
4 stalks celery
⅓ cup olive oil
freshly ground black pepper
1 cup chopped onion
1 × 14 oz can peeled tomatoes, drained
1 tablespoon tomato paste
2–3 tablespoons wine vinegar
2 tablespoons sugar
2 tablespoons drained capers
12 small green olives, pitted
1 tablespoon pine nuts

Cut the aubergines (eggplants) into 1 cm/½ inch dice, put into a colander, sprinkle generously with salt and leave to drain. After about 30 minutes rinse in cold water and pat dry with kitchen paper towels.

Cover the celery with cold water, bring to the boil and simmer for 5 minutes, then drain and cut into 5 mm/¼ inch dice.

Heat 3 × 15 ml spoons/3 tablespoons oil in a frying pan (skillet) and fry the aubergine (eggplant) cubes fairly briskly, stirring and turning frequently, for about 10 minutes, until golden and tender. Season with salt and pepper.

Heat the remaining oil in a pan and fry the onion gently for 5 minutes. Add the celery, stir and fry for 5 minutes. Press the tomatoes through a coarse strainer into the pan and stir in the tomato purée (paste) and a little salt and pepper. Simmer very gently for 10 minutes or until the celery is tender, then add 2 × 15 ml spoons/2 tablespoons vinegar, the sugar, capers, olives, pine nuts and aubergine (eggplant) cubes. Stir, then simmer for a few minutes.

Taste and adjust the seasoning, adding extra vinegar and salt and pepper to taste. Leave to become cold then store in the refrigerator.

Pile into a serving dish and serve cold, either alone or surrounded with tuna fish and quartered hard-boiled (hard-cooked) eggs.

SERVES 4

# SPAGHETTI ALLA SIRACUSANA

*Spaghetti Syracuse Style*

Sicilians are very fond of combining pasta with well flavoured vegetable sauces. You can vary this typical recipe according to the vegetables available, using courgettes (zucchini) instead of aubergine (eggplant) for instance.

**Metric/Imperial**

1 medium green pepper
1 medium aubergine
1 × 400 g/14 oz can peeled tomatoes
4 × 15 ml spoons/4 tablespoons olive oil
2 cloves garlic, sliced
12 small black olives, stoned
1 × 15 ml spoon/1 tablespoon drained capers
3 anchovy fillets, finely chopped
1 × 15 ml spoon/1 tablespoon chopped fresh basil or rosemary
freshly ground black pepper
salt
350 g/12 oz spaghetti
50 g/2 oz Pecorino Sardo or Parmesan cheese, grated

**American**

1 medium green pepper
1 medium eggplant
1 × 14 oz can peeled tomatoes
¼ cup olive oil
2 cloves garlic, sliced
12 small ripe olives, pitted
1 tablespoon drained capers
3 anchovy fillets, finely chopped
1 tablespoon chopped fresh basil or rosemary
freshly ground black pepper
salt
¾ lb spaghetti
½ cup grated Pecorino Sardo or Parmesan cheese

Caponata, Spaghetti alla Siracusana

Grill (broil) the pepper under a medium heat, turning frequently, until the skin is charred and can be peeled off. Halve, deseed and rinse the pepper to remove all traces of skin and seeds. Cut into 5 mm/¼ inch dice.

Cut the aubergine (eggplant) into 1 cm/½ inch dice. Drain and roughly chop the tomatoes. Heat the oil and garlic gently in a saucepan until the oil is well flavoured. Discard the garlic. Add the aubergine (eggplant) and fry gently, stirring frequently, for 10 minutes. Add the tomatoes, diced green pepper, olives, capers, anchovies, herbs, black pepper and salt to taste. Stir, cover and simmer while cooking the spaghetti.

Put the spaghetti, upright, into a large pan of boiling salted water (it will slide into the water as it softens), and boil steadily for about 10 minutes or until *al dente*. Drain thoroughly, put into a hot serving dish and add the cheese and the hot sauce. Toss together lightly and serve immediately.

SERVES 4

## TONNINO AL POMODORO ALLE SARDE

*Fresh Tuna Fish Sardinian Style*

A great deal of Sardinian cooking is done over an open fire. This typical fish dish can be cooked outdoors or indoors, and any firm fish can be used instead of tuna.

**Metric/Imperial**
4 tuna fish steaks, 2.5 cm/1 inch thick
salt
*freshly ground black pepper*
*flour for dusting*
3 × 15 ml spoons/3 tablespoons olive oil
1 small onion, chopped
1 clove garlic, crushed
0.75 kg/1½ lb tomatoes, skinned
2 × 15 ml spoons/2 tablespoons chopped fresh parsley
1 bay leaf
4 anchovy fillets, mashed
few black olives

**American**
4 tuna fish steaks, 1 inch thick
salt
*freshly ground black pepper*
*flour for dusting*
3 tablespoons olive oil
1 small onion, chopped
1 clove garlic, crushed
1½ lb tomatoes, skimmed
2 tablespoons chopped fresh parsley
1 bay leaf
4 anchovy filets, mashed
few ripe olives

Season the fish with salt and pepper and dust with flour. Heat 2 × 15 ml spoons/2 tablespoons oil in a large shallow pan and fry the fish quickly until golden each side, then transfer to a plate.

Add the remaining oil to the pan and fry the onion and garlic gently for 5 minutes. Meanwhile press the tomatoes through a coarse strainer or purée in an electric blender. Add the parsley, bay leaf and anchovy to the pan and stir for a few seconds. Add the tomatoes, bring to the boil and continue boiling until the mixture has reduced to a thin sauce consistency. Season with pepper, replace the fish and simmer gently for 15 minutes, turning the tuna steaks once during cooking.

Turn off the heat, add the olives and leave for 5 minutes before serving.

SERVES 4

Tonnino al Pomodoro alle Sarde

# POMODORI AL PANE

## Stuffed Tomatoes

These tomatoes make a marvellous accompaniment to roast chicken, lamb or pork. Alternatively add 4 finely chopped anchovy fillets and 1 × 15 ml spoon/1 tablespoon capers to the filling and serve the tomatoes as a course on their own.

**Metric/Imperial**

4 large tomatoes
salt
freshly ground black pepper
50 g/2 oz fresh breadcrumbs
1 small onion, coarsely grated
2 cloves garlic, crushed
50 g/2 oz mushrooms, finely chopped
2 × 5 ml spoons/2 teaspoons sugar
1 × 15 ml spoon/1 tablespoon chopped fresh parsley
few basil leaves, finely chopped, or a large pinch of dried basil
2 × 15 ml spoons/2 tablespoons olive oil
4 black olives

**American**

4 large tomatoes
salt
freshly ground black pepper
1 cup fresh bread crumbs
1 small onion, coarsely grated
2 cloves garlic, crushed
½ cup finely chopped mushrooms
2 teaspoons sugar
1 tablespoon chopped fresh parsley
few basil leaves, finely chopped, or a large pinch of dried basil
2 tablespoons olive oil
4 ripe olives

Cut the tomatoes horizontally in half and scoop out the insides. Season the halves with salt and pepper and turn upside down on a plate to drain while preparing the stuffing.

Chop the tomato pulp and put into a basin with the breadcrumbs, onion, garlic, mushrooms, sugar, parsley and basil. Season well with salt and pepper; mix thoroughly.

Pile into the tomato halves, arrange in a well oiled ovenproof dish and sprinkle a little olive oil over each. Bake uncovered in a preheated moderate oven (180°C/350°F, Gas Mark 4) for about 30 minutes until cooked but still firm. Serve hot, garnished with a whole or halved black (ripe) olive.
SERVES 4

Tonno Sott' Olio con Cipolle

# TONNO SOTT' OLIO CON CIPOLLE

## Tuna Fish Salad

A simple and colourful starter.

**Metric/Imperial**

1 × 200 g/7 oz can tuna fish
freshly ground black pepper
2 × 5 ml spoons/2 teaspoons drained capers
2 tomatoes, thinly sliced
1 small mild onion, finely sliced
squeeze of lemon juice

**American**

1 × 7 oz can tuna fish
freshly ground black pepper
2 teaspoons drained capers
2 tomatoes, thinly sliced
1 small mild onion, finely sliced
squeeze of lemon juice

Drain the tuna fish, reserving 1 × 15 ml spoon/1 tablespoon of the oil. Crumble the fish with a fork and arrange in piles in the centre of shallow individual serving dishes.

Sprinkle with black pepper and the capers. Surround with slices of tomato topped with onion. Add the lemon juice to the reserved oil and sprinkle a little over each portion.
SERVES 3

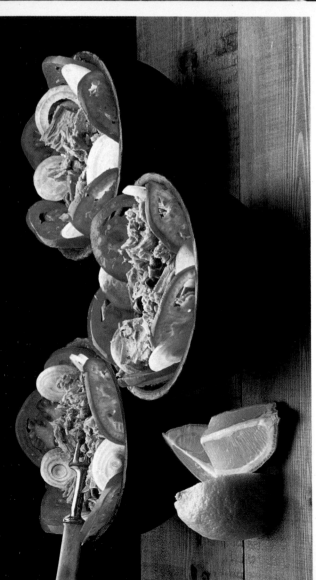

# SARDE RIPIENE ALLA PALERMITANA

*Sardines Stuffed Palermo Style*

Fresh sardines are often available in Soho, but small herring or mackerel would be equally acceptable cooked with this sweet, crunchy stuffing.

**Metric/Imperial**

12 large fresh sardines
6 anchovy fillets, finely chopped
50 g/2 oz pine nuts
50 g/2 oz sultanas
large pinch of sugar
pinch of grated nutmeg
1 × 15 ml spoon/1 tablespoon chopped
  fresh parsley
freshly ground black pepper
olive oil for sprinkling
12 bay leaves
50 g/2 oz fresh breadcrumbs
juice of 1 lemon
TO GARNISH:
parsley sprigs
lemon slices

**American**

12 large fresh sardines
6 anchovy filets, finely chopped
¼ cup pine nuts
⅓ cup seedless white raisins
large pinch of sugar
pinch of grated nutmeg
1 tablespoon chopped fresh parsley
freshly ground black pepper
olive oil for sprinkling
12 bay leaves
1 cup fresh bread crumbs
juice of 1 lemon
TO GARNISH:
parsley sprigs
lemon slices

Cut the heads off the sardines, open down the belly and remove the gut and backbone. Wash in cold water and pat dry. Mix together the anchovy fillets, pine nuts, sultanas (seedless white raisins), sugar, nutmeg, parsley, pepper to taste, and 1 × 15 ml spoon/1 tablespoon oil. Fill each sardine with a little of the mixture, reshape and arrange in an oiled ovenproof dish.

Arrange a bay leaf between each fish and sprinkle liberally with breadcrumbs then oil. Cook in a preheated moderately hot oven (190°C/375°F, Gas Mark 5) for about 30 minutes, until cooked and lightly browned.

Sprinkle with lemon juice and serve in the same dish, garnished with parsley and lemon.
SERVES 4

Pomodori al Pane, Coniglio con Olive Verdi (page 15)

# FARSUMAGRU

## *Stuffed Meat Roll*

Although this meat roll takes a little time to prepare, it is worth the trouble because it makes an original, very tasty and not too expensive meal for about 8 people. Any leftovers are delicious eaten cold with salad.

### Metric/Imperial

0.5 kg/1¼ lb topside of beef, cut as one
    1 cm/½ inch thick slice
salt
freshly ground black pepper
50 g/2 oz crustless bread
milk for soaking
225 g/8 oz minced shoulder of pork
225 g/8 oz minced lean beef
2 eggs, lightly beaten
40 g/1½ oz Parmesan or Pecorino cheese,
    finely grated
1 × 15 ml spoon/1 tablespoon chopped
    fresh parsley
2 hard-boiled eggs, coarsely chopped
50 g/2 oz salami or cooked ham,
    coarsely chopped
50 g/2 oz Caciocavallo or Provolone or
    Gruyère cheese, coarsely chopped
2 × 15 ml spoons/2 tablespoons olive oil
1 small onion, sliced
150 ml/¼ pint coarse red wine
1 × 15 ml spoon/1 tablespoon tomato
    purée
4 × 15 ml spoons/4 tablespoons hot
    water

### American

1¼ lb top round of beef, cut as one
    ½ inch thick slice
salt
freshly ground black pepper
2 oz crustless bread
milk for soaking
1 cup ground shoulder of pork
1 cup ground lean beef
2 eggs, lightly beaten
⅓ cup finely grated Parmesan or
    Pecorino cheese
1 tablespoon chopped fresh parsley
2 hard-cooked eggs, coarsely chopped
¼ cup coarsely chopped salami or
    processed ham
¼ cup coarsely chopped Caciocavallo or
    Provolone or Gruyère cheese
2 tablespoons olive oil
1 small onion, sliced
⅔ cup coarse red wine
1 tablespoon tomato paste
¼ cup hot water

Lay the slice of meat on a working surface and flatten it out with a rolling pin. Continue beating until the meat is about 5 mm/¼ inch thick and measures about 23 × 25 cm/9 × 10 inches. Season with salt and pepper.

Soak the bread in a little milk, and when

softened squeeze it dry and beat it with a fork. Add the pork, beef, beaten eggs, Parmesan or Pecorino cheese, parsley, and salt and pepper to taste. Mix until thoroughly blended. Spread this mixture over the flattened meat to within 2.5 cm/1 inch of the edges.

Mix together the chopped eggs, salami or ham, and the Caciocavallo or Provolone or Gruyère cheese and arrange down the centre of the meat. Starting from the shorter edge, roll up neatly to form a thick sausage shape and tie securely with string.

Heat the oil in a flameproof casserole and fry the onion gently for a few minutes. Put in the meat roll and fry, turning occasionally, until lightly browned all over. Add the wine, the tomato purée (paste) blended with the hot water, and a little salt and pepper. Cover tightly and simmer very gently for 1½ to 2 hours until tender, turning once and adding a little more hot water if too much of the liquid evaporates.

Transfer the meat roll to a carving board and remove the strings. Skim the fat off the pan juices then boil the juices rapidly until reduced to a sauce consistency. Carve the meat in thick slices, arrange on a hot dish and spoon over the sauce.

SERVES 8

# POLPETTE ALLA CASALINGA

## *Homestyle Meat Balls*

Throughout Italy, light, well seasoned, fried meat balls are a favourite and very delicious way of making small amounts of meat feed large families. In Sicily, the polpette are often served in a tomato sauce.

### Metric/Imperial

tomato sauce (see page 28)
50 g/2 oz crustless white bread
milk for soaking
0.5 kg/1 lb pie veal or boneless leg of
    beef
2 cloves garlic
small bunch of parsley leaves
2 thin strips of lemon rind
2 eggs
25 g/1 oz Parmesan cheese, grated
large pinch of grated nutmeg
salt
freshly ground black pepper
flour for coating
oil for shallow frying

### American

tomato sauce (see page 28)
2 oz crustless white bread
milk for soaking
1 lb pie veal or boneless leg of beef
2 cloves garlic
small bunch of parsley leaves
2 thin strips of lemon rind
2 eggs
¼ cup grated Parmesan cheese
large pinch of grated nutmeg
salt
freshly ground black pepper
flour for coating
oil for shallow frying

Prepare the tomato sauce. Break the bread into a basin, barely cover with milk and leave to stand for 10 minutes or until softened, then squeeze to remove liquid.

Trim the meat of any skin or gristle and cut into pieces. Pass the meat, bread, garlic, parsley and lemon rind through a fine mincer (grinder) twice. Beat in the eggs, cheese, nutmeg and salt and pepper to taste and mix thoroughly.

With well-floured hands, shape the mixture into small balls, about 2.5cm/1 inch in diameter then roll on a floured surface and flatten slightly with a knife. Handle as little as possible so that the meat balls remain light.

Heat enough oil in a large frying pan (skillet) to give a depth of 5 mm/¼ inch. Fry the meat balls in batches, for about 3 minutes on each side until crisp outside and cooked through. Lift out and drain on crumpled kitchen paper towels.

While the meat balls are frying, reheat the tomato sauce, diluting it with water to give a fairly thin consistency. Put in the meat balls, stir gently and simmer for 15 to 20 minutes until hot through.

SERVES 4 TO 5

# CONIGLIO CON OLIVE VERDI

*Rabbit with Green Olives*

Olives, herbs and capers give the rabbit a delicious flavour in this authentic Sicilian recipe.

**Metric/Imperial**
1 plump young rabbit, jointed
1 × 15 ml spoon/1 tablespoon olive oil
100 g/4 oz belly pork, diced
225 g/8 oz onions, thickly sliced
2 sticks celery, thickly sliced
1 × 15 ml spoon/1 tablespoon flour
450 ml/¾ pint stock or water
1 bay leaf
1 small sprig of rosemary
salt
freshly ground black pepper
50 g/2 oz green olives, stoned
1 × 15 ml spoon/1 tablespoon drained
capers (optional)

**American**
1 plump young rabbit, jointed
1 tablespoon olive oil
¼ lb salt pork, diced
½ lb onions, thickly sliced
2 stalks celery, thickly sliced
1 tablespoon all-purpose flour
2 cups stock or water
1 bay leaf
1 sprig of rosemary
salt
freshly ground black pepper
⅓ cup pitted green olives
1 tablespoon drained capers (optional)

Wash and dry the pieces of rabbit. Put the oil, pork, onions and celery into a large flameproof casserole and heat gently, stirring now and then, until the fat runs from the pork. Add the rabbit and fry gently, turning, until lightly browned, about 10 minutes.

Sprinkle in the flour and stir for 1 minute. Stir in the hot stock or water, bay leaf, rosemary, and salt and pepper to taste. Bring to the boil, cover tightly and simmer until the rabbit is tender, 45 minutes to 1 hour. Add the olives, and capers if used, and simmer for 10 minutes.

SERVES 4

# AGNELLO IN UMIDO ALLA SARDA

*Leg of Lamb Stewed Sardinian Style*

Shepherds tending their flocks sometimes cook outdoors. This way of simmering lamb is ideal for campfire cookery, or for anyone with limited cooking facilities.

**Metric/Imperial**
3–4 large cloves garlic
sprigs of fresh rosemary
1 small leg of lamb
salt
freshly ground black pepper
3 × 15 ml spoons/3 tablespoons olive oil
1 small onion, chopped
1 kg/2 lb tomatoes, skinned and chopped
4 × 15 ml spoons/4 tablespoons water

**American**
3–4 large cloves garlic
sprigs of fresh rosemary
1 small leg of lamb
salt
freshly ground black pepper
3 tablespoons olive oil
1 small onion, chopped
4 cups skinned and chopped tomatoes
¼ cup water

Cut the garlic cloves into thin slivers and divide the rosemary into tiny sprigs. Rub the lamb all over with salt and pepper. With a pointed knife make small incisions all over the surface and insert a sliver of garlic and a sprig of rosemary in each.

Heat the oil in a flameproof casserole, add the lamb and fry, turning frequently, until lightly browned. Lower the heat, add the onion and fry gently for a few minutes. Add the tomatoes and water, bring to the boil and season to taste. Cover the casserole tightly and simmer gently until the lamb is tender, allowing 20 minutes per 0.5 kg/1 lb plus 20 minutes.

Transfer the lamb to a hot dish. If necessary, skim any excess fat from the surface of the tomato liquid and boil rapidly, uncovered, until reduced to a sauce consistency. Check the seasoning. Serve with the meat, using any leftover sauce to moisten a dish of pasta.

SERVES 6 TO 8

Farsumagru, Polpette alla Casalinga

# CASSATA ALLA SICILIANA

*Sicilian Celebration Gâteau*

The famous *cassata* was originally a celebration cake before it became widely available in the now popular ice cream form. There are many versions of the gâteau, the base of which is a *pan di Spagna* (Italian sponge cake) made in an oblong, round or basin shape.

**Metric/Imperial**

ITALIAN SPONGE CAKE:
4 eggs, separated
150 g/5 oz caster sugar
finely grated rind of ½ lemon
75 g/3 oz plain flour
25 g/1 oz cornflour
2 × 15 ml spoons/2 tablespoons warm water

FILLING AND TOPPING:
0.75 kg/1½ lb Ricotta or curd cheese
175 g/6 oz caster sugar
5–6 × 15 ml spoons/5–6 tablespoons orange liqueur
50 g/2 oz plain chocolate, finely chopped
75 g/3 oz candied peel, finely chopped

TO DECORATE:
glacé fruits (optional)
strips of candied peel
coarsely grated chocolate

**American**

ITALIAN SPONGE CAKE:
4 eggs, separated
⅔ cup sugar
finely grated rind of ½ lemon
¾ cup all-purpose flour
¼ cup cornstarch
2 tablespoons warm water

FILLING AND TOPPING:
1½ lb Ricotta or curd cheese
¾ cup sugar
5–6 tablespoons orange liqueur
2 squares semi-sweet chocolate, finely chopped
½ cup finely chopped candied peel

TO DECORATE:
candied fruits (optional)
strips of candied peel
coarsely grated chocolate

Put the egg yolks, sugar and lemon rind into a large mixing bowl and beat until pale. Lightly fold in flour and cornflour (cornstarch), a little at a time, then add the water. Whisk the egg whites until stiff but not dry and fold into the cake mixture very lightly, but thoroughly.

Turn the mixture into a greased and floured deep cake tin (springform pan) of about 1.75 litre/3 pint/7½ cup capacity. Bake in the centre of a preheated moderate oven (180°C/350°F, Gas Mark 4) for 45 to 50 minutes, until firm to the touch. Cool on a wire rack.

To make the filling and topping, press the cheese through a sieve (strainer) into a basin, add the sugar and 2 × 15 ml spoons/2 tablespoons liqueur and beat until light and fluffy. Put half of this mixture into the refrigerator to chill for the topping. Add the chocolate and peel to the remainder and mix well.

Cut the sponge cake horizontally into 3 layers. Place one layer on a serving dish, sprinkle with liqueur and spread with half of the filling. Cover with a second layer of sponge, sprinkle with liqueur and spread with the rest of the filling. Place the remaining layer of sponge on top. Press the layers together firmly and chill the cake in the refrigerator.

An hour or so before serving, spread the topping evenly over the top and sides of the cake. Finish the cake with a decorative arrangement of glacé (candied) fruits if used, and peel; sprinkle the top with coarsely grated chocolate.

SERVES 8

# ZABAGLIONE

This most famous of all Italian desserts is very quick and simple to make, but make it immediately before serving as it is apt to separate if left to stand for more than a few minutes. A superb light dessert to complete a meal.

**Metric/Imperial**

4 egg yolks
4 × 15 ml spoons/4 tablespoons caster sugar
1 × 15 ml spoon/1 tablespoon warm water
7 × 15 ml spoons/7 tablespoons sweet Marsala

TO SERVE:
sponge fingers

**American**

4 egg yolks
¼ cup sugar
1 tablespoon warm water
7 tablespoons sweet Marsala

TO SERVE:
lady fingers

Place the egg yolks, sugar and warm water in a basin over a saucepan of hot water. Beat with a balloon or rotary whisk (not an electric beater) until pale in colour and frothy.

Whisk in the Marsala a little at a time and continue whisking over heat until the mixture increases in volume, becomes thick and foamy and holds its shape in a spoon, about 5 to 10 minutes.

Remove from the heat immediately and spoon into tall wine glasses. Serve with sponge fingers (lady fingers).

SERVES 3 TO 4

# MANTECATO DI PESCHE

*Peach Water Ice*

A typical Sicilian fruit-based water ice. Melon ice is equally delicious made the same way, replacing the peaches with 0.75 kg/1½ lb ripe, peeled and deseeded Cantaloup flesh.

**Metric/Imperial**

100 g/4 oz sugar
150 ml/¼ pint water
4 large peaches
juice of 1 lemon

**American**

¼ cup sugar
⅔ cup water
4 large peaches
juice of 1 lemon

# GRANITA DI CAFFÈ

*Coffee Water Ice*

A wonderfully refreshing ice for a very hot day, but only if made from an infusion of freshly ground good quality coffee beans.

**Metric/Imperial**
150 g/5 oz finely ground continental roast coffee
75 g/3 oz caster sugar
1 litre/1¾ pints boiling water
TO SERVE:
whipped cream (optional)
finely ground coffee (optional)

**American**
2½ cups finely ground continental roast coffee
6 tablespoons sugar
4¼ cups boiling water
TO SERVE:
whipped cream (optional)
finely ground coffee (optional)

Put the coffee and sugar into a warmed earthenware jug and pour the boiling water over it. Cover and stand the jug in a saucepan of boiling water and leave to infuse for 20 to 30 minutes. Cool.

When cold, strain through a filter paper. Pour into a shallow tray and freeze, without stirring, until frozen to a granular but solid mush.

Serve in tall glasses, with a spoon, either plain or topped with a whirl of whipped cream and a sprinkling of finely ground coffee.

SERVES 4 TO 6

Mantecato di Pesche, Granita di Caffè (left); Cassata alla Siciliana (below).

Put the sugar and water into a small saucepan and heat gently until the sugar has completely dissolved, then boil fast for 5 minutes. Leave until quite cold.

Immerse the peaches in boiling water for 1 minute, then drain and remove skin and stones (seeds). Without delay, purée the flesh in an electric blender or pass through a nylon sieve (strainer). Immediately mix thoroughly with the lemon juice to prevent discolouration. Stir in the cold syrup, pour into a shallow freezer tray and freeze until firm.

When partially frozen, turn into a basin and whisk vigorously for a few minutes, then return to the tray and freeze until firm.

An hour before serving, transfer to the centre of the refrigerator to allow the ice to soften a little. To serve; scoop the water ice into glasses or sundae dishes.

SERVES 4

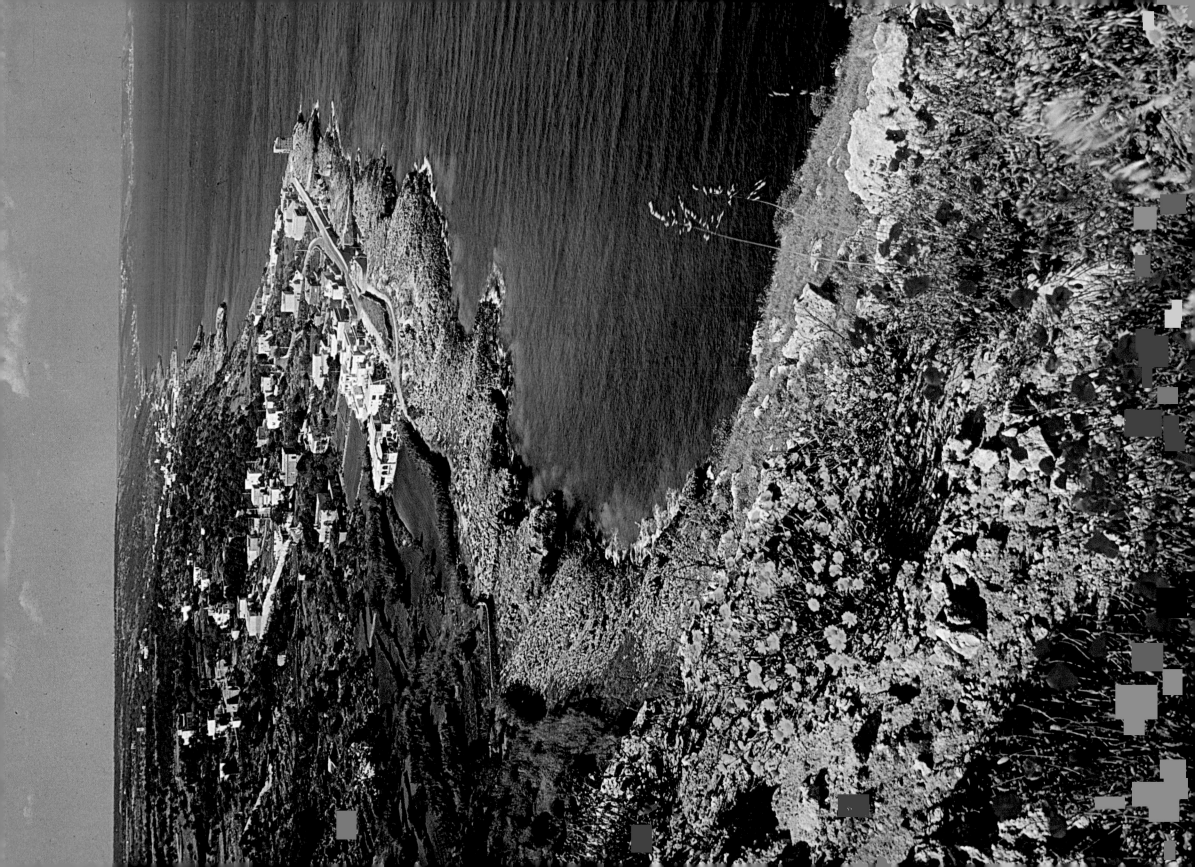

# Apulia, Basilicata & Calabria

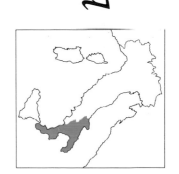

Together these three regions form the rugged 'foot' of Southern Italy, with Apulia forming the heel, Basilicata the high arch and Calabria the extended toe.

Apulia, bounded on one coastline by the Adriatic and by the gulf of Taranto on the other, has a very equable climate and large areas of arable land producing an abundance of fresh fruit and vegetables. Apulians are said to be the champion pasta eaters of Italy, and they claim to have invented several pasta shapes, including *ricchietelle*. The sauce served with these 'little ears' gets caught inside the crevices making, so the Apulians claim, a much tastier dish! Another pasta, *turcinielli*, is in the form of little macaroni spirals.

Both pastas are served with tomato or meat sauce, often with vegetables added and grated cheese. Apulian versions of pizza include *calzoni* – 'trousers' of pasta stuffed with onions, anchovies and olives, while around Lecce the pizza are topped with fried mushrooms as well as tomatoes. The long coastline yields a rich harvest of colourful fish, and Taranto is noted for its oyster and mussel beds. The local fish soup is considered one of the best in Italy, containing a variety of fish, shellfish and spices.

Basilicata is a very mountainous region and it is not surprising that the cooking is robust and frugal. Sheep and pigs are reared in large numbers. The lamb often has a natural flavour of herbs, and herbs generally feature strongly in local cooking. Pig products, including sausages, are often smoked and preserved in traditional ways. Game and chicken are popular, and in the mountains cabbage and pork soup is comforting food on a winter night. Ginger is used in many dishes with the object, it is said, of creating thirst – doubtless for the rough wines produced on the steep mountain slopes. Dairy products, including various kinds of cheese, are plentiful. Much of the cheese finds its way into robust pasta dishes, and these are popular.

With its extensive coastline, Calabria is renowned for its fish soups and *fritto misto*. Fresh tuna fish, sardines, cod, clams and anchovies all abound. Vegetables grow profusely, and the climate is particularly favourable for aubergine (eggplant), peppers and mushrooms, a fact reflected in the wide variety of recipes featuring these vegetables, and in the Calabrians' fondness for soup. The mainstay of all inland family meals is likely to be a vegetable soup thickened with pasta. Meat is not renowned for its quality in this area, but local chefs make some unusual dishes from veal, lamb, kid, hare, rabbit, chicken and guinea fowl. Offal (variety meat) is cooked in tomato sauce, and juniper berries are a popular flavouring. In Calabria, pasta has acquired some odd shapes and evocative names, names that can be roughly translated as 'ladies' curls', 'priests' ears' and 'angels' hair', for example.

Throughout the South, pastry shops are filled with little cakes, biscuits (cookies), and sweetmeats, many of them specialities made for a particular festival or Saint's Day. Honey, nuts and spices are popular flavourings in these treats.

# FUNGHI RIPIENI

*Stuffed Mushrooms*

When large cap mushrooms are available, stuffed mushrooms make a pleasant meal starter or an ideal vegetable to serve with chicken, fish or lamb.

**Metric/Imperial**

12 large cup-shaped mushrooms
olive oil
1 medium onion, finely chopped
1 clove garlic, crushed
40 g/1½ oz fresh breadcrumbs
2 × 15 ml spoons/2 tablespoons chopped
    fresh parsley
50 g/2 oz cooked ham, chopped
2 × 15 ml spoons/2 tablespoons grated
    Parmesan cheese
salt
freshly ground black pepper
finely chopped fresh parsley to garnish

**American**

12 large cup-shaped mushrooms
olive oil
1 medium onion, finely chopped
1 clove garlic, crushed
¾ cup fresh bread crumbs
2 tablespoons chopped fresh parsley
¼ cup chopped processed ham
2 tablespoons grated Parmesan cheese
salt
freshly ground black pepper
finely chopped fresh parsley to garnish

Remove and chop the mushroom stalks.

Heat 3 × 15 ml spoons/3 tablespoons olive oil in a small saucepan and fry the onion and garlic gently for 5 minutes. Stir in the breadcrumbs and fry for 2 to 3 minutes until crisp. Add the parsley, mushroom stalks, ham, cheese and salt and pepper to taste. Mix well.

Lightly oil the base of a shallow oven-proof dish and arrange the mushrooms, cup side up, in a single layer in the dish. Put a little filling in each mushroom and sprinkle liberally with oil.

Cover loosely with a piece of grease-proof (waxed) paper and bake in a pre-heated moderately hot oven (190°C/375°F, Gas Mark 5) for 20 to 30 minutes. Sprinkle chopped parsley over the mushrooms to garnish.

SERVES 4

# PEPERONI CON TONNO E CAPPERI

*Sweet Peppers with Tuna Fish and Capers*

For preference, choose red and yellow sweet peppers for a colourful antipasto, but if not available green peppers will do.

**Metric/Imperial**

6 large sweet peppers
4 × 15 ml spoons/4 tablespoons olive oil
squeeze of lemon juice
1 clove garlic, crushed (optional)
salt
freshly ground black pepper
1 × 200 g/7 oz can tuna fish, drained
1–2 × 15 ml spoons/1–2 tablespoons
    drained capers
parsley sprigs to garnish

**American**

6 large sweet peppers
¼ cup olive oil
squeeze of lemon juice
1 clove garlic, crushed (optional)
salt
freshly ground black pepper
1 × 7 oz can tuna fish, drained
1–2 tablespoons drained capers
parsley sprigs to garnish

Grill (broil) the large sweet peppers under a moderate heat, turning from time to time, until the skins are charred and blistered all over, about 10 minutes. When cool enough to handle, peel off the skins, then cut each sweet pepper lengthwise into three strips and discard the stem, pith and seeds. Rinse under cold water to remove all traces of skin and seeds.

Put the strips in a basin with the oil, lemon juice, garlic (if used) and a little salt and pepper. Leave to marinate for 30 minutes, stirring occasionally. Drain, re-serving the marinade. Lay the pepper strips flat.

Flake the tuna fish and mix in the capers. Place a generous spoonful on each pepper strip and roll up. Arrange the rolls in a shallow serving dish with the colours alternating. Pour the marinade over and serve garnished with parsley.

SERVES 6

*Funghi Ripieni*

# INSALATA DI POMODORI

*Tomato Salad*

The qualities Italians look for in a tomato salad are a crisp texture and a fresh flavour. The crispness comes from using under-ripe, slightly green tomatoes, and the freshness from a generous sprinkling of fresh herbs.

**Metric/Imperial**
6 large firm tomatoes
1 clove garlic, crushed
3 × 15 ml spoons/3 tablespoons olive oil
salt
freshly ground black pepper
TO GARNISH:
chopped fresh basil or parsley and green spring onion tops

**American**
6 large firm tomatoes
1 clove garlic, crushed
3 tablespoons olive oil
salt
freshly ground black pepper
TO GARNISH:
chopped fresh basil or parsley and green scallion tops

Wash and dry the tomatoes and chill in the refrigerator until required. Cut into 5 mm/¼ inch thick slices and arrange on a shallow dish, slightly over-lapping.

Mix together the garlic, oil and a generous seasoning of salt and pepper, and spoon over the tomatoes. Scatter the garnish over and serve.

SERVES 4

# INSALATA DI CAVOLFIORE

*Cauliflower Salad*

This colourful salad makes a good antipasto on its own, or as an accompaniment to thinly sliced salami or Mortadella.

**Metric/Imperial**
1 large, firm white cauliflower
salt
juice of ½ lemon or 1½ × 15 ml spoons/
  1½ tablespoons wine vinegar
freshly ground black pepper
4–5 × 15 ml spoons/4–5 tablespoons
  olive oil
6 anchovy fillets, finely chopped
1–2 × 15 ml spoons/1–2 tablespoons
  drained capers

**American**
1 large, firm white cauliflower
salt
juice of ½ lemon or 1½ tablespoons wine
  vinegar
freshly ground black pepper
¼–⅓ cup olive oil
6 anchovy fillets, finely chopped
1–2 tablespoons drained capers
⅓ cup small ripe olives

Cut away the outside leaves and hard stalk from the cauliflower and break into florets. Drop into boiling salted water and cook until just tender but still quite firm, about 5 minutes. Drain, rinse under cold water and drain again.

In a salad bowl mix together the lemon juice or vinegar, a little salt and pepper, and the oil. Add the cauliflower and toss gently to coat with the dressing. Sprinkle with the anchovies, capers and parsley and serve surrounded with the olives.

SERVES 4

Peperoni con Tonno e Capperi, Insalata di Cavolfiore

1 × 15 ml spoon/1 tablespoon chopped
  fresh parsley
50 g/2 oz small black olives

*Apulia, Basilicata & Calabria*

## COZZE GRATINATE

*Mussel Antipasto*

A dish to be enjoyed in coastal resorts all around Italy, but nowhere better than Taranto which is famous for its mussel beds. Serve as a hot antipasto or as a fish course.

**Metric/Imperial**
2.25 litres/4 pints fresh mussels
40 g/1½ oz fresh white breadcrumbs
2 large cloves garlic, finely chopped
25 g/1 oz fresh parsley, finely chopped
freshly ground black pepper
4 × 15 ml spoons/4 tablespoons olive oil

**American**
5 pints fresh mussels
¾ cup fresh white bread crumbs
2 large cloves garlic, finely chopped
¾ cup finely chopped fresh parsley
freshly ground black pepper
¼ cup olive oil

Scrape the mussels carefully in cold water, discarding any that do not shut tightly when given a sharp tap, then wash them thoroughly.

Put the drained mussels into a heavy based saucepan, cover and place over a high heat for 5 to 6 minutes, shaking the pan frequently, until the mussel shells open. Remove from the heat, lift off and discard the top shells, leaving each mussel in its lower shell. Arrange these side by side in a large shallow gratin dish or in 4 individual gratin dishes.

Quickly mix together the breadcrumbs, garlic, parsley and a little pepper, and sprinkle over the mussels. Sprinkle the oil evenly over the top. Place in a pre-heated hot oven (230°C/450°F, Gas Mark 8) for 5 minutes, until the crumbs are just tinged brown. Take care not to overcook and toughen the mussels. Alternatively, brown under a preheated grill (broiler).
SERVES 4

## MELANZANE AL FUNGHETTO

*Aubergine (Eggplant) Fried in Oil*

A simple way of cooking aubergine (eggplant) to serve as a vegetable with meat or chicken.

**Metric/Imperial**
2 medium aubergines
salt
6 × 15 ml spoons/6 tablespoons olive oil
2 cloves garlic, chopped
freshly ground black pepper
2 × 15 ml spoons/2 tablespoons chopped fresh parsley

**American**
2 medium eggplants
salt
6 tablespoons olive oil
2 cloves garlic, chopped
freshly ground black pepper
2 tablespoons chopped fresh parsley

Wipe the aubergines (eggplants) and remove the stalks, but do not peel. Cut into 1 cm/½ inch dice, put in a colander, sprinkle with salt and leave to drain for 1 hour. Pat dry with kitchen paper towels.

Heat the oil in a large frying pan (skillet), then add the garlic and aubergine (eggplant). Fry gently, stirring now and then, for 15 to 20 minutes, or until tender; during this time the aubergine (eggplant) will absorb the oil.

Season with pepper, stir in the parsley and serve hot.
SERVES 3 TO 4

## ZITA ALLA CALABRESE

*Savoury Macaroni*

A robust pasta dish popular in the Southern regions. Zita is a type of short-cut macaroni, either straight or curved, but any tubular pasta cut in short lengths can be used. If Caciocavallo cheese is not available, use mature Provolone instead.

**Metric/Imperial**
3 × 15 ml spoons/3 tablespoons olive oil
2 cloves garlic, crushed
1 medium onion, chopped
1 small chilli pepper, seeded and finely chopped
4 rashers smoked streaky bacon, chopped
1 × 400 g/14 oz can peeled tomatoes, chopped
salt
225 g/8 oz zita or short-cut pasta
50 g/2 oz Caciocavallo cheese, grated

**American**
3 tablespoons olive oil
2 cloves garlic, crushed
1 medium onion, chopped
1 small chili pepper, seeded and finely chopped
4 slices bacon, chopped
1 × 14 oz can peeled tomatoes
salt
2 cups zita or short-cut pasta
½ cup grated Caciocavallo cheese

Heat 2 × 15 ml spoons/2 tablespoons olive oil in a saucepan and fry the garlic, onion, chilli pepper and bacon together very gently for about 10 minutes, stirring occasionally. Add the tomatoes and their liquid with salt to taste and bring to the boil. If necessary break up the tomatoes with a wooden spoon. Cover the pan and simmer for 20 minutes.

Cook the pasta in plenty of fast boiling, well salted water until just cooked but still firm, about 8 to 10 minutes. Drain thoroughly. Pour the remaining oil into a hot serving dish and put in alternate layers of pasta, sauce and cheese, finishing with a layer of cheese.

Serve immediately, or cover and leave the flavours to blend in a cool oven until ready to serve.
SERVES 3 TO 4

## SEDANI AL FORNO

*Celery with Tomatoes and Bacon*

Celery can take a long time to become really tender in the oven, so cook this tasty dish in the oven at the same time as a casserole or braise. Once cooked it reheats well.

**Metric/Imperial**
2 medium heads of celery
juice of ½ lemon
salt
5 × 15 ml spoons/5 tablespoons olive oil
1 medium onion, sliced
4 rashers streaky bacon, chopped
freshly ground black pepper
1 × 400 g/14 oz can peeled tomatoes, chopped
chopped fresh parsley to garnish

**American**
2 medium heads of celery
juice of ½ lemon
salt
⅓ cup olive oil
1 medium onion, sliced
4 slices bacon, chopped
freshly ground black pepper
1 × 14 oz can peeled tomatoes, chopped
chopped fresh parsley to garnish

Trim the celery and separate the stalks, discarding any that are tough or bruised. Wash and cut into 7.5 cm/3 inch lengths. Put into a saucepan and cover with cold water. Add the lemon juice and 1 × 5 ml spoon/1 teaspoon salt. Bring to the boil and simmer for 15 minutes, then drain.

Heat 3 × 15 ml spoons/3 tablespoons oil in a large, shallow flameproof casserole and fry the onion and half of the bacon slowly for 5 minutes. Add the drained celery with salt and pepper to season, stir and fry for 3 to 4 minutes.

Add the remaining bacon, then the tomatoes and their juice, and finally the rest of the olive oil. Cover tightly and cook in a preheated moderate oven (180°C/350°F, Gas Mark 4) until tender, about 1 to 1½ hours. Sprinkle with parsley.
SERVES 4

Sedani al Forno, Cozze Gratinate

# SALSA DI CARNE

*Meat Sauce*

When small amounts of meat have to feed large families, a meat sauce served with pasta or *gnocchi* is a favourite Italian way of giving everyone a fair share. If there's a bottle of dry red or white wine open, replace some of the stock with wine. Another optional addition is chopped mushrooms.

**Metric/Imperial**

3 × 15 ml spoons/3 tablespoons olive oil
100 g/4 oz onion, finely chopped
100 g/4 oz carrot, finely chopped
1 stick celery, finely chopped
1 clove garlic, crushed
1 × 15 ml spoon/1 tablespoon chopped fresh parsley
0.5 kg/1 lb minced beef
2 × 15 ml spoons/2 tablespoons flour
450 ml/¾ pint beef stock
1 × 15 ml spoon/1 tablespoon tomato purée
salt
freshly ground black pepper

Triglie alla Calabrese

**American**

3 tablespoons olive oil
1 cup finely chopped onion
1 cup finely chopped carrot
1 celery stalk, finely chopped
1 clove garlic, crushed
1 tablespoon chopped fresh parsley
2 cups ground beef
2 tablespoons all-purpose flour
2 cups beef stock
1 tablespoon tomato paste
salt
freshly ground black pepper

Heat the oil in a heavy based saucepan and fry the vegetables, garlic and parsley gently until beginning to soften and turn golden. Add the meat, increase the heat, and fry, stirring, until the meat changes colour from red to grey.

Sprinkle in the flour, stir and fry for 1 to 2 minutes, then stir in the stock, tomato purée (paste) and salt and pepper to taste. Simmer very gently, uncovered, for 45 minutes to 1 hour, stirring occasionally. By that time the sauce should be well reduced but not too thick. Season to taste and serve with pasta or as required.
SERVES 6

# TRIGLIE ALLA CALABRESE

*Red Mullet (Snapper) Calabrian Style*

**Metric/Imperial**

4 red mullet, each weighing about 225 g/8 oz
salt
2 × 15 ml spoons/2 tablespoons olive oil
1 × 15 ml spoon/1 tablespoon chopped fresh marjoram or 1 × 5 ml spoon/1 teaspoon dried marjoram
40 g/1½ oz butter
2 × 15 ml spoons/2 tablespoons drained capers
12 black olives, stoned and slivered
thinly pared zest of ½ lemon, shredded
1 × 15 ml spoon/1 tablespoon chopped fresh parsley

**American**

2 red snapper, each weighing about 1 lb
salt
2 tablespoons olive oil
1 tablespoon chopped fresh marjoram or 1 teaspoon dried marjoram
3 tablespoons butter
2 tablespoons drained capers
12 ripe olives, pitted and slivered
thinly pared zest of ½ lemon, shredded
1 tablespoon chopped fresh parsley

Ask the fishmonger to gut and clean the fish, leaving the liver and head in place. Wash the fish, pat dry and sprinkle the insides with salt.

Heat the oil and marjoram in a large, heavy frying pan (skillet), and fry the mullet (snapper) over moderate heat for 6 to 8 minutes each side, turning once.

Meanwhile, heat the butter in a small saucepan until it begins to smell 'nutty' and turn brown, then remove from the heat and stir in the capers, olives, lemon zest and parsley.

Carefully transfer the cooked fish to a hot serving dish, and pour the hot sauce over the fish.
SERVES 4

# POLLO CON OLIVE

*Sautéed Chicken with Olives*

A useful all-in-one-pan way of making a tasty dish from oven-ready chicken. Under various names, and with slight variations such as the addition of green peppers, mushrooms, green olives, red wine or anchovy fillets, it is found all over Italy.

**Metric/Imperial**
1.75 kg/4 lb chicken, cut into 6 portions
seasoned flour for coating
3 × 15 ml spoons/3 tablespoons olive oil
1 large onion, chopped
1–2 cloves garlic, crushed
1 bay leaf
150 ml/¼ pint dry white wine
1 × 400 g/14 oz can peeled tomatoes
1 × 15 ml spoon/1 tablespoon tomato purée
12 black olives
freshly ground black pepper
salt (optional)
fresh parsley to garnish

**American**
4 lb chicken, cut into 6 portions
seasoned flour for coating
3 tablespoons olive oil
1 large onion, chopped
1–2 cloves garlic, crushed
1 bay leaf
⅔ cup dry white wine
1 × 14 oz can peeled tomatoes
1 tablespoon tomato paste
12 ripe olives
freshly ground black pepper
salt (optional)
fresh parsley to garnish

Wash and dry the chicken joints and dust lightly with seasoned flour. Heat the oil in a flameproof casserole and fry the chicken until golden all over; transfer to a plate.

Add the onion to the casserole and fry gently for 5 minutes, then add the garlic and bay leaf and fry for 1 minute. Pour in the wine and simmer for 1 to 2 minutes, then add the tomatoes and their juice and the tomato purée (paste). Bring to the boil, breaking up the tomatoes if whole, replace the chicken and add the olives. Cover the casserole and simmer gently, stirring occasionally, for 45 minutes or until the chicken is tender.

Transfer the chicken to a serving dish, boil the sauce rapidly, uncovered, to concentrate the flavour and thicken the sauce. Remove the bay leaf, adjust the seasoning and pour the sauce over the chicken. Snip a little parsley over the surface before serving.
SERVES 6

*Pollo con Olive*

# NOCCIOLETTE

*Hazelnut (Filbert) Sweets*

**Metric/Imperial**
75 g/3 oz hazelnuts
100 g/4 oz butter
40 g/1½ oz icing sugar
1½ × 15 ml spoons/1½ tablespoons honey
100 g/4 oz plain flour
icing sugar for dusting

**American**
¾ cup filberts
½ cup butter
⅓ cup confectioners' sugar
1½ tablespoons honey
1 cup all-purpose flour
confectioners' sugar for dusting

Set the oven to 180°C/350°F, Gas Mark 4. Spread the hazelnuts (filberts) on a baking sheet and put into the oven for 6 to 8 minutes until lightly toasted. Remove from the oven and rub in a coarse cloth to remove the brown skins, then grind the nuts, but not too finely.

Cream the butter, sugar and honey together until light and fluffy, then stir in the flour and nuts, mixing to a smooth dough. With lightly floured hands, pinch off pieces of dough the size of walnuts and shape into ovals. Arrange these on greased baking sheets, about 2.5 cm/1 inch apart.

Bake in the preheated oven for about 15 minutes, until firm. Cool slightly and roll in icing (confectioners') sugar.
MAKES ABOUT 24

*Nocciollette*

# Campania

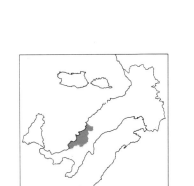

Those who have spent holidays in the sunny bay of Naples will know that the people are cheerful, gregarious and easy going and are said to sing their way through all kinds of adversity. The historical background of the area is one of poverty rather than affluence, and their cooking reflects the necessity of making the most of foods that happen to be available locally. The cuisine, like the people, is colourful and full of character, and like the other Southern regions is based largely on the plentiful use of tomatoes, garlic, olive oil, herbs, anchovies, cheese and fresh fish and vegetables. Because of its fertile volcanic soil, the Romans called the area Campania Felix, the happy country.

Citrus fruits, nuts, vines and olives are widely cultivated and men, women and children can be seen tilling, tending and harvesting crops of vegetables between the trees and on every spare piece of land. Courgettes (zucchini), sweet peppers, beans, aubergines (eggplants), potatoes, root and salad vegetables and herbs all flourish in the soil and sunny climate.

Naples is the culinary capital of the area and boasts the invention of both the pizza and tubular pasta. The latter, of which spaghetti and macaroni are typical, is manufactured in vast quantities both for home consumption and export. Throughout the area you will find pizzas galore, from light and dainty single portion *pizzette* to gigantic pizza sold by the metre from huge baking sheets. A never-to-be-forgotten sight is the fabulous orange glow inside a traditional brick-lined pizza oven aflame with olive and lemon wood. The aromatic ashes are raked out before the pizzas are put in to cook.

Campania is the home of Mozzarella cheese, still occasionally made from buffalo milk but more often nowadays from cows' milk. Mozzarella should be eaten very fresh and dripping with whey. Just off the square in Sorrento you can visit a dairy and see Treccia, a variety of Mozzarella, being made. Local gourmets become lyrical when describing the charm of fresh Treccia, seasoned with black pepper and eaten with raw broad beans (lima beans) and wholewheat bread.

Rice is not eaten much in the South, but Campania has one great rice speciality called *sartu*, a versatile dish of boiled rice layered with tomato sauce and a variety of meat and vegetable ingredients, the latter varying according to taste, budget, or simply which foods happen to be available. Many other specialities are based on tomato sauces, and ripe tomatoes are bottled and preserved in vast quantities for use throughout the winter.

Although grapes grow prolifically and pleasant local wines can be found, few of these have become known beyond Campania. When visiting the area, your best plan is to taste and try, not forgetting the wines of Ischia and Capri. The Neapolitans share with the Sicilians the credit for having introduced ice cream to the rest of Europe and the name of Tortoni is still celebrated. Throughout the Southern regions all those with a sweet tooth will find their tastes well catered for in the bars and pastry shops.

# PEPERONI GRATINATI 'O PARRUCCHIANO

*Stuffed Peppers au Gratin*

Sweet green and red peppers stuffed in various ways are popular throughout Southern Italy. This recipe for a cold antipasto is a speciality of the attractive 'O Parracchiano' restaurant in Sorrento.

**Metric/Imperial**
1 medium aubergine, peeled
salt
4 large green peppers
1 large slice firm bread, 5 mm/¼ inch thick
150 ml/¼ pint olive oil (approximately)
2 cloves garlic, crushed
4 anchovy filets, finely chopped
12 large black olives, stoned and chopped
1 × 15 ml spoon/1 tablespoon rinsed and drained capers
1 × 15 ml spoon/1 tablespoon chopped fresh basil
1 × 15 ml spoon/1 tablespoon chopped fresh parsley
freshly ground black pepper
TOPPING:
2 × 15 ml spoons/2 tablespoons dried breadcrumbs
1 × 15 ml spoon/1 tablespoon chopped fresh parsley
1 large clove garlic, crushed

**American**
1 medium eggplant, peeled
salt
4 large green peppers
1 large slice firm bread, ¼ inch thick
⅔ cup olive oil (approximately)
2 cloves garlic, crushed
4 anchovy filets, finely chopped
12 large ripe olives, pitted and chopped
1 tablespoon rinsed and drained capers
1 tablespoon chopped fresh basil
1 tablespoon chopped fresh parsley
freshly ground black pepper
TOPPING:
2 tablespoons dried bread crumbs
1 tablespoon chopped fresh parsley
1 large clove garlic, crushed

Cut the aubergine (eggplant) into 5 mm/¼ inch dice, put into a colander, sprinkle with salt and leave to drain for 1 hour.

Grill (broil) the peppers under a moderate heat, turning frequently, for about 10 minutes or until the skins are blistered and blackened all over. When cool enough to handle, remove the stem, peel off the skin, cut the peppers in half lengthwise and discard the seeds. Rinse under cold water to remove all traces of skin and seeds.

---

# SALSA DI POMODORO – 1

*Tomato Sauce – using Fresh Tomatoes*

A fresh tasting tomato sauce to make when tomatoes are plentiful.

**Metric/Imperial**
0.75 kg/1½ lb tomatoes, roughly chopped
1 small onion, finely chopped
1 small carrot, finely chopped
1 stick celery, chopped
1 × 5 ml spoon/1 teaspoon sugar
salt
freshly ground black pepper
chopped fresh basil or parsley to serve

**American**
3 cups roughly chopped tomatoes
1 small onion, finely chopped
1 small carrot, finely chopped
1 stalk celery, chopped
1 teaspoon sugar
salt
freshly ground black pepper
chopped fresh basil or parsley to serve

Place the tomatoes in a saucepan with the onion, carrot, celery, sugar and salt and pepper to taste. Simmer for 20 to 30 minutes until the tomatoes have reduced almost to a purée. Press through a sieve (strainer). If a thicker sauce is required, return to the pan and boil briskly, uncovered, until reduced to the desired consistency.

Check the seasoning and stir in the herbs just before serving.

MAKES ABOUT 450 ML/¾ PINT (2 CUPS) SAUCE

# SALSA DI POMODORO – 2

*Tomato Sauce – using Canned Tomatoes*

A richly flavoured, rough textured sauce that need not be sieved unless a smooth sauce is required.

**Metric/Imperial**
2 × 15 ml spoons/2 tablespoons oil
1 large clove garlic, halved
1 × 400 g/14 oz can peeled tomatoes
1 × 15 ml spoon/1 tablespoon tomato purée
2 × 5 ml spoons/2 teaspoons sugar
salt
freshly ground black pepper

**American**
2 tablespoons oil
1 large clove garlic, halved
1 × 14 oz can peeled tomatoes
1 tablespoon tomato paste
2 teaspoons sugar
salt
freshly ground black pepper

Heat the oil and garlic in a saucepan over low heat for 5 minutes or until the oil is well flavoured. Discard the garlic.

Add the tomatoes and their liquid, tomato purée (paste), sugar and salt and pepper to taste. Bring to the boil, cover and simmer very gently for at least 40 minutes, preferably longer.

Beat the sauce if necessary to break up any large pieces of tomato, check the seasoning and use as required.

MAKES ABOUT 300 ML/½ PINT (1¼ CUPS) SAUCE

Rinse the aubergine (eggplant) cubes in cold water and pat dry with kitchen paper towels. Remove the crusts and cut the bread into 5 mm/¼ inch dice.

Heat 2 × 15 ml spoons/2 tablespoons oil in a large frying pan (skillet) and fry the bread cubes until crisp, stirring frequently. Transfer to a mixing bowl. Heat another 3 × 15 ml spoons/3 tablespoons oil in the same pan and fry the aubergine (eggplant) cubes until golden, then add to the bread.

Heat another 2 × 15 ml spoons/2 tablespoons oil in the pan and fry the garlic very gently for 2 to 3 minutes, then stir in the anchovies, olives, capers, basil and parsley. Fry for 1 minute and then add to the bread and aubergine (eggplant) with pepper to taste; mix well.

Lay the peppers flat, divide the stuffing between them, roll up and place in a well oiled shallow baking dish. Mix the topping ingredients together and sprinkle evenly over the peppers. Sprinkle each pepper liberally with oil and bake in a preheated moderate oven (180°C/350°F, Gas Mark 4) for 30 to 40 minutes. Serve cold.
SERVES 4

Zuppa di Zucchini (below); Salsa di Pomodoro (above left)

# ZUPPA DI ZUCCHINI
Courgette (Zucchini) Soup

A nourishing yet delicately flavoured country soup. Although prettily flecked with flakes of egg, it can be reheated the following day provided it does not boil.

**Metric/Imperial**
0.75 kg/1½ lb courgettes
50 g/2 oz butter
1 medium onion, sliced
1.75 litres/3 pints water
2 chicken stock cubes
2 eggs
3 × 15 ml spoons/3 tablespoons grated Parmesan cheese
2 × 15 ml spoons/2 tablespoons chopped fresh basil or parsley
salt
freshly ground black pepper
TO SERVE:
grated Parmesan cheese

**American**
1½ lb zucchini
¼ cup butter
1 medium onion, sliced
7½ cups water
2 chicken bouillon cubes
2 eggs
3 tablespoons grated Parmesan cheese
2 tablespoons chopped fresh basil or parsley
salt
freshly ground black pepper
TO SERVE:
grated Parmesan cheese

Top and tail the courgettes (zucchini) and cut into 5 mm/¼ inch slices. Melt the butter in a large saucepan and fry the onion very gently for 5 minutes. Add the courgettes (zucchini) and fry, stirring frequently, for 5 to 10 minutes until lightly golden. Add the water, crumble in the stock (bouillon) cubes, bring to the boil, cover and simmer gently for about 20 minutes.

Pass the mixture through the coarse mesh of a mouli-légume or sieve, or purée in an electric blender, then return to the saucepan. Just before serving bring the soup to the boil.

Put the eggs, cheese and herbs in the bottom of a large warmed soup tureen and, using a wire whisk, beat together thoroughly. Still whisking, pour the boiling soup slowly onto the beaten eggs. Check the seasoning and serve immediately. Pass a bowl of Parmesan cheese separately.
SERVES 6 TO 8

# PIZZA ALLA NAPOLETANA

*Neapolitan Style Pizza*

Commercial pizzas made with ordinary bread dough toughen as they cool and cannot be reheated. But at.Le Alexide hotel on the water's edge at Vico Equense, the chef showed me this special way of making a featherlight pizza which both reheats and freezes well.

## Metric/Imperial

PIZZA DOUGH:
15 g/½ oz fresh yeast
2 × 15 ml spoons/2 tablespoons warm
  water
225 g/8 oz plain flour
1 × 5 ml spoon/1 teaspoon salt
2 × 15 ml spoons/2 tablespoons olive oil
3 × 15 ml spoons/3 tablespoons milk
  (approximately)

TOPPING:
350 g/12 oz tomatoes, skinned and
  seeded, or 1 × 400 g/14 oz can peeled
  tomatoes, drained
175 g/6 oz Mozzarella or Bel Paese or
  Primula cheese
4 × 15 ml spoons/4 tablespoons olive oil
salt
freshly ground black pepper
1 × 15 ml spoon/1 tablespoon chopped
  fresh basil
1 × 5 ml spoon/1 teaspoon dried
  oregano
4 × 15 ml spoons/4 tablespoons grated
  Parmesan cheese

## American

PIZZA DOUGH:
¼ cake compressed yeast
2 tablespoons warm water
2 cups all-purpose flour
1 teaspoon salt
2 tablespoons olive oil
3 tablespoons milk (approximately)

TOPPING:
¾ lb tomatoes, skinned and seeded, or
  1 × 14 oz can peeled tomatoes,
  drained
6 oz Mozzarella or Bel Paese or Primula
  cheese
¼ cup olive oil
salt
freshly ground black pepper
1 tablespoon chopped fresh basil
1 teaspoon dried oregano
¼ cup grated Parmesan cheese

Blend the yeast with the warm water. Sift the flour and salt into a heap on a working surface, make a well in the centre and pour in the yeast, oil and milk.

With the fingers of one hand, gradually draw the flour into the liquids and mix to form a stiff but pliable dough, adding a little more milk if necessary.

Knead the dough, slapping it vigorously on the working surface and rolling it around under the palm of your hand, for at least 5 minutes. Gather into a ball, place in an oiled basin, cover and leave to rise until doubled in bulk. This will take about 1 hour in a warm place or 2 to 3 hours at room temperature.

While the dough is rising, prepare the topping. Cut the tomatoes into thin strips, or chop the canned tomatoes. Cut the cheese into small slices.

When the dough is risen, turn it on to a floured surface and divide into 2 or 4 pieces, depending on the size of pizzas required. Knead each piece lightly and place on well oiled aluminium pie plates, either two 20–23 cm/8–9 inch plates or four 15–18 cm/6–7 inch plates. With floured knuckles press out the dough to cover the base of the plates and reach 1 cm/½ inch up the sides.

Brush with oil, cover with the tomatoes and season well with salt and pepper. Sprinkle with the basil and oregano. Place the cheese slices on top and sprinkle with

Parmesan. Sprinkle oil liberally over each pizza. Leave to rise in a warm place for 30 minutes.

Bake in a preheated hot oven (220°C/ 425°F, Gas Mark 7) for 15 minutes, then reduce the heat to moderate (180°C/ 350°F, Gas Mark 4) and bake for another 5 to 10 minutes, until the pizzas are cooked through.

SERVES 4 TO 8

The small pizzas are usually considered single portion size, but the large ones can be cut into 3 or 4 portions each.

*To freeze:* prepare the pizzas to the baking stage, open freeze then wrap and label. To reheat, unwrap and cook from frozen, starting in a cold oven set to heat to 230°C/450°F, Gas Mark 8. Bake for 25 to 40 minutes, depending on size.

*Alternative toppings:* using the same tomato base, with or without the cheese, add one or several of the following: anchovy fillets, black olives, sliced sautéed mushrooms, salami or sausage slices, peeled shrimps or thinly sliced green peppers.

*Pizza alla Napoletana*

# VERMICELLI CON LE COZZE

*Vermicelli with Tomato and Mussel Sauce*

This classic recipe from the Bay of Naples can be made with either mussels or *vongole* (a type of small clam) or a mixture of the two. Either vermicelli or spaghetti can form the pasta base but the customary grated cheese is not served with this dish.

**Metric/Imperial**

2.25 litres/4 pints fresh mussels
150 ml/¼ pint water
5 × 15 ml spoons/5 tablespoons olive oil
1 medium onion, finely chopped
2 cloves garlic, sliced
0.75 kg/1½ lb tomatoes, skinned and chopped
350 g/12 oz vermicelli or spaghetti
salt
freshly ground black pepper
2 × 15 ml spoons/2 tablespoons chopped fresh parsley

**American**

5 pints fresh mussels
⅔ cup water
⅓ cup olive oil
1 medium onion, finely chopped
2 cloves garlic, sliced
3 cups skinned and chopped tomatoes
¾ lb vermicelli or spaghetti
salt
freshly ground black pepper
2 tablespoons chopped fresh parsley

Scrub and scrape the mussels and wash thoroughly, discarding any that do not close tightly when sharply tapped. Put into a large pan with the water and heat briskly, shaking the pan occasionally, for 5 to 6 minutes or until the shells open. Remove from the heat and drain off the water. Set aside a few of the mussels in their shells to garnish. Discard the shells from the rest of the mussels.

Heat 3 × 15 ml spoons/3 tablespoons of the oil in a large saucepan and fry the onion until soft and golden. Stir in the garlic, then the tomatoes. Simmer gently for about 30 minutes until the tomatoes have reduced to a pulp.

Cook the pasta in plenty of boiling salted water until just tender, about 10 minutes. Drain thoroughly, put into a hot dish containing the remaining oil and toss until lightly coated.

Season the sauce with salt and pepper, add the shelled mussels and heat through, stirring.

Pile the sauce on top of the pasta. Serve immediately, garnished with the reserved mussels and chopped parsley.

SERVES 4

*Vermicelli con le Cozze*

# SPAGHETTATA

*Spaghetti with Oil and Garlic*

This centuries-old way of serving pasta with an oil and garlic dressing has acquired a new name and a new role. Around the Bay of Naples, *spaghettata* is now the smart way of sobering up your guests for their hazardous journey home and bringing the party to a close.

**Metric/Imperial**

350 g/12 oz spaghetti, trenette or linguine
salt
5 × 15 ml spoons/5 tablespoons olive oil
2 large cloves garlic, crushed
freshly ground black pepper
2 × 15 ml spoons/2 tablespoons finely chopped fresh parsley

**American**

¾ lb spaghetti, trenette or linguine
salt
⅓ cup olive oil
2 large cloves garlic, crushed
freshly ground black pepper
2 tablespoons finely chopped fresh parsley

Cook the pasta in plenty of well salted boiling water for about 10 minutes, or until just cooked but still firm. Drain thoroughly.

In the same pan, heat the oil and garlic together very gently for about 5 minutes. When the oil is well flavoured add several grinds of pepper and the chopped parsley.

Return the drained pasta to the pan and toss lightly, with 2 forks, until all the strands of pasta are glistening with oil and well flavoured with garlic. Serve at once in soup plates.

SERVES 4

# BRACIOLETTE RIPIENI

*Stuffed Veal Rolls*

This recipe needs small seamless escallopes (scallops) of milk-fed veal, which can be beaten out very thinly.

**Metric/Imperial**

8 escallopes of veal, each weighing 50 g/2 oz

8 thin pieces cooked bacon or ham

25 g/1 oz crustless bread

3 × 15 ml spoons/3 tablespoons sultanas

25 g/1 oz pine nuts or blanched slivered almonds

4 × 15 ml spoons/4 tablespoons grated Parmesan cheese

2 × 15 ml spoons/2 tablespoons chopped fresh parsley

salt

freshly ground black pepper

1 × 15 ml spoon/1 tablespoon olive oil

150 ml/¼ pint white wine

**American**

8 scallops of veal, each weighing 2 oz

8 thin pieces cooked bacon or processed ham

1 oz crustless bread

3 tablespoons seedless white raisins

¼ cup pine nuts or blanched slivered almonds

¼ cup grated Parmesan cheese

2 tablespoons chopped fresh parsley

salt

freshly ground black pepper

1 tablespoon olive oil

⅔ cup white wine

Lay the escallopes (scallops) flat between greaseproof (waxed) paper and beat until thin but unbroken. Remove the paper and lay a slice of bacon or ham on each.

Soak the bread in water and then squeeze dry. Put into a basin and add the sultanas (seedless white raisins), nuts, cheese, parsley and salt and pepper to taste; mix well. Divide the stuffing between the slices of veal, roll up, and secure with wooden cocktail sticks (toothpicks).

Heat the oil in a sauté pan and fry the rolls fairly briskly, turning until lightly browned all over. Pour the wine over the rolls, cover tightly and simmer very gently for 20 to 25 minutes until tender, turning once. If more convenient, cook in a preheated moderate oven (180°C/350°F, Gas Mark 4).

Transfer the rolls to a serving dish. Boil the pan juices until reduced by about half and thickened. Remove the cocktail sticks (toothpicks) from the rolls and serve with the reduced pan juices poured over. Crusty bread makes a good accompaniment.

SERVES 4

# ROGNONI TRIFOLATI

*Sautéed Veal Kidneys*

In this recipe the rapid cooking of the sliced veal kidneys prevents them toughening or drying.

32

## [Rognoni Trifolati]

**Metric/Imperial**
0·5 kg/1¼ lb veal kidneys, with fat
covering removed
1 large clove garlic, halved
1 × 15 ml spoon/1 tablespoon oil
25 g/1 oz butter
2 × 15 ml spoons/2 tablespoons
chopped fresh parsley
juice of ½ large lemon
salt
freshly ground black pepper
TO GARNISH:
small triangles of crisp fried bread

**American**
1¼ lb veal kidneys, with fat covering
removed
1 large clove garlic, halved
1 tablespoon oil
2 tablespoons butter
2 tablespoons chopped fresh parsley
juice of ½ large lemon
salt
freshly ground black pepper
TO GARNISH:
small triangles of crisp fried bread

With a sharp knife, peel away the thin membrane covering the kidneys and remove the core. Slice the kidneys very thinly.

Put the garlic, oil and butter into a large frying pan (skillet) and heat very gently for about 2 minutes until the garlic flavours the oil. Discard the garlic.

Increase the heat, and when the fat is hot add the kidney slices and fry briskly, tossing and stirring constantly for about 2 minutes. Stir in the parsley and continue cooking and stirring for 2 minutes. Add the lemon juice and cook for 1 to 2 minutes, until the kidney slices are tender but still juicy and slightly pink in the centre, and the small amount of liquid is syrupy.

Season with salt and pepper and serve immediately, garnished with triangles of fried bread.
SERVES 4

*Braciolette Ripieni, Rognoni Trifolati (left); Bistecca alla Pizzaiola (above)*

# BISTECCA ALLA PIZZAIOLA
*Beef Steak with Fresh Tomato Sauce*

Pizzaiola sauce is always made with fresh tomatoes, cooked briefly until soft but not pulped, and heavily flavoured with garlic and fresh herbs. It is a good sauce for improving the eating quality of less tender steaks or chops and is excellent with portions of fried white fish.

**Metric/Imperial**
4 rib or rump steaks, 2 cm/¾ inch thick
salt
freshly ground black pepper
olive oil
SAUCE:
2 × 15 ml spoons/2 tablespoons olive oil
3 cloves garlic, sliced
0.5 kg/1¼ lb tomatoes, skinned, seeded and chopped
fresh basil leaves or dried oregano
parsley sprigs to garnish (optional)

**American**
4 rib or rump steaks, ¾ inch thick
salt
freshly ground black pepper
olive oil
SAUCE:
2 tablespoons olive oil
3 cloves garlic, sliced
2½ cups skinned, seeded and chopped tomatoes
fresh basil leaves or dried oregano
parsley sprigs to garnish (optional)

Beat the steaks to tenderize and season with salt and pepper. Sprinkle with oil and leave to stand.

To prepare the sauce, heat the oil and garlic gently in a saucepan for 1 to 2 minutes, then add the tomatoes with salt and pepper to taste. Bring to the boil and cook briskly for 5 to 6 minutes, until the tomatoes are just softened. Add a few roughly broken basil leaves or 1 × 1.25 ml spoon/¼ teaspoon dried oregano.

Oil the base of a large sauté pan and fry the steaks briskly for 2 minutes on each side, until lightly browned. Top each steak with a thick layer of the sauce, cover the pan tightly and cook over a low heat for 6 to 10 minutes or until the steaks are tender and cooked according to taste.

Snip a little parsley over the steaks if liked, and serve very hot.
SERVES 4

# BISQUIT TORTONI ALLA MANDORLA

*Ice Cream with Toasted Almonds*

A very simple ice cream, frozen conveniently in individual dishes ready to serve.

**Metric/Imperial**
40 g/1½ oz flaked almonds
1 large egg white
300 ml/½ pint double cream
4 × 15 ml spoons/4 tablespoons icing
  sugar, sifted
3 × 15 ml spoons/3 tablespoons brandy
  or liqueur

**American**
⅓ cup slivered almonds
1 egg white
1¼ cups heavy cream
½ cup confectioners' sugar, sifted
3 tablespoons brandy or liqueur

and fry a single layer of aubergine (eggplant) slices over a moderately high heat until lightly browned on both sides, then drain on kitchen paper towels. Continue frying the aubergine (eggplant) slices in batches, adding oil as necessary.

Cut the Mozzarella, Bel Paese or Primula cheese into thin slices. Oil a shallow oven-to-table dish of about 1.75 litres/3 pints (7½ cup) capacity. Cover the bottom of the dish with a thin layer of tomato sauce and add a layer of fried aubergine (eggplant) slices. Spoon over more tomato sauce, top with half of the cheese pieces and sprinkle with half of the Parmesan. Repeat the layers.

Bake in the centre of a preheated moderately hot oven (200°C/400°F, Gas Mark 6) for 25 to 30 minutes, until bubbling hot and golden.
SERVES 6

Melanzane alla Parmigiana (left)

# MELANZANE ALLA PARMIGIANA

*Aubergine (Eggplant), Cheese and Tomato Pie*

The secret of this succulent dish, good enough to eat on its own or as a vegetable accompaniment, is plenty of tomato sauce and freshly grated Parmesan cheese.

**Metric/Imperial**
450 ml/¾ pint tomato sauce (see page 28)
1 kg/2 lb aubergines, peeled
salt
flour for dusting
5–8 × 15 ml spoons/5–8 tablespoons
  olive oil
175 g/6 oz Mozzarella, Bel Paese or
  Primula cheese
50 g/2 oz Parmesan cheese, freshly
  grated

**American**
2 cups tomato sauce (see page 28)
2 lb eggplants, peeled
salt
flour for dusting
⅓–½ cup olive oil
6 oz Mozzarella, Bel Paese or Primula
  cheese
½ cup freshly grated Parmesan cheese

Prepare the tomato sauce. Cut the aubergines (eggplants) lengthwise into 5 mm/¼ inch slices. Put them in a colander with a generous sprinkling of salt between each layer, cover and leave to drain for 1 hour. Press each slice between kitchen paper towels to dry thoroughly and then dust lightly with flour.

Heat about 3 × 15 ml spoons/3 tablespoons oil in a large frying pan (skillet),

Spread the almonds thinly on a baking sheet and grill (broil) under moderate heat, tossing frequently, until lightly toasted. Leave to cool.

Whisk the egg white until stiff but not dry. In another basin, whisk the cream until beginning to thicken, then add half the sugar and half the brandy or liqueur and whisk until thick. Repeat with the remaining sugar and brandy. Lightly but thoroughly fold in the egg white.

Spoon the mixture into 6 to 8 ice cream paper cases or freezerproof sundae glasses and top with the toasted almonds. Place in deep baking tins and cover loosely with foil so that the ices are covered but not flattened. Freeze for about 3 hours or until firm.

About 30 minutes before serving, transfer from the freezer to the refrigerator to allow the ices to soften a little before serving.

SERVES 6 TO 8

## PASTIERA ALLA NAPOLETANA

*Neapolitan Curd Tart*

A deliciously flavoured filling baked in a buttery, lemon-flavoured shortcrust pastry (basic pie dough) which Italians call *pasta frolla*.

Serve as a dessert or as a mid-morning treat with coffee.

### Metric/Imperial

PASTA FROLLA:
225 g/8 oz plain flour
pinch of salt
75 g/3 oz caster sugar
100 g/4 oz butter, softened
finely grated rind of ½ lemon
2 egg yolks
CURD FILLING:
350 g/12 oz Ricotta or curd cheese
75 g/3 oz caster sugar
3 eggs, well beaten
50 g/2 oz blanched almonds, finely chopped
75 g/3 oz candied peel, finely chopped
finely grated rind of ½ lemon
finely grated rind of ½ orange
1 × 2.5 ml spoon/½ teaspoon vanilla essence
icing sugar for dusting

### American

PASTA FROLLA:
2 cups all-purpose flour
pinch of salt
6 tablespoons sugar
¼ cup butter, softened
finely grated rind of ½ lemon
2 egg yolks

*Pastiera alla Napoletana*

Sift flour, salt and sugar together in a heap on a working surface and make a well in the centre. Put the butter, lemon rind and egg yolks into the well.

With the fingertips, gradually draw the flour into the centre and mix all the ingredients to a firm, smooth dough. Wrap the pastry in foil and chill in the refrigerator for 1 hour.

To make the filling, rub the Ricotta cheese through a sieve (strainer) into a basin and beat in the sugar. Gradually beat in the eggs, followed by all the remaining ingredients except the icing (confectioners') sugar. Mix well.

Roll out the pastry thinly and use to line an 18–20 cm/7–8 inch fan ring, reserving the trimmings for the decoration. Fill the flan with the cheese mixture and smooth the surface. Roll out the pastry trimmings thinly, cut into 1 cm/½ inch wide strips with a fluted roller and use to make a criss-cross pattern over the top of the flan.

Bake for about 45 minutes in the centre of a preheated moderate oven (180°C/350°F, Gas Mark 4). Cool on a wire rack. Serve cold, dusted with icing (confectioners') sugar.

MAKES 6 SLICES

*Bisquit Tortoni alla Mandora*

CURD FILLING:
¾ lb Ricotta or curd cheese
6 tablespoons sugar
3 eggs, well beaten
½ cup finely chopped blanched almonds
½ cup finely chopped candied peel
finely grated rind of ½ lemon
finely grated rind of ½ orange
¼ teaspoon vanilla extract
confectioners' sugar for dusting

# Lazio, Abruzzi & Molise

These three regions straddle the centre of Italy and form a kind of divide between the colourful, tasty, olive oil and tubular pasta dishes of the South and the rather more sophisticated butter and flat pasta dishes of the North. Lazio, with its long coastline bulging gently into the Tyrrhenian Sea, and Abruzzi and Molise with their Adriatic seaboards meet in the Appenine Mountains which form the backbone of Italy.

Rome is the capital of Lazio, and as all roads lead to Rome it is not surprising that the cooking of all Italy, and of the world, is to be found there. Yet Rome has a native culinary tradition of its own. To find it you must forsake the international tourist *ristoranti* and seek the simpler *trattorie* and *osterie* where the Romans themselves eat and where the cooking is more akin to that of a private home. In such eating places you will find the dishes simple, robust, aromatic and often highly seasoned. The pasta dishes are more likely to follow the flat pasta tradition of Northern Italy, but there are also many excellent tubular pasta specialities involving spaghetti and macaroni. The ribbon pasta of Rome, known as *fettucine*, is often served simply *al burro* (with butter) or *alla panna* (with butter and cream), leaving the diner to add grated Parmesan cheese to his taste. Rome is also known for its delicate cannelloni dishes, made in the Northern style by stuffing flat rectangles of pasta. One of the Roman specialities is *abbacchio* (unweaned baby lamb).

Festivals are celebrated with enthusiasm and each has its gastronomic traditions – goat at Easter, stuffed spit-roasted pig for the Festa di Noantri, snails in highly flavoured sauces for Midsummer Night, and eels and stuffed capon at Christmas. The new season's young, tender vegetables are given the special care they deserve, resulting in delectable dishes such as fried baby artichokes, button onions in sweet-sour sauce and peas with prosciutto.

The cooking of Abruzzi and Molise is robust and reflects the varied landscape and the food it produces. Pigs reared in the mountains provide pork for the country hams, garlic sausages and a spicy form of mortadella. The pigs' livers are made into liver sausages flavoured with orange rind and garlic. Milk from sheep provides Ricotta cheese. Both sea and river fish are plentiful and coastal towns offer their own variety of *brodetto* (fish soup), often flavoured with the white vinegar produced in Abruzzi. A regional speciality is *scapece*, a dish of fried marinated fish, made in much the same way as the Lombardy marinated fish (see page 81) but using a higher proportion of vinegar. Another regional fish dish, octopus and cuttlefish cooked in a hot red chilli sauce, is aptly named *polpipi in purgatorio*.

Pasta is generally of the Southern tubular variety, but Abruzzi has its own speciality *maccheroni alla chitarra*. This is a thick ribbon pasta made by pressing the dough –through wires stretched at narrow intervals across the special guitar-shaped loom found in many homes. Only a little local wine is produced in Abruzzi and Molise, but Lazio produces considerable quantities of light wines around the picturesque castle villages of the Alban Hills and around Lake Bolsena. The best known are Frascati and Est! Est! Est!

# SUPPLÌ AL TELEFONO

### Rice Balls with Cheese

Mozzarella cheese is used in these rice balls so that when the *supplì* are cut open the cheese extends into long 'wires'. The risotto for this dish can be freshly made and cooled, or leftover as long as it is not too dry.

**Metric/Imperial**

2 eggs
*cold risotto, made with 350 g/12 oz rice (see page 82)*
100 g/4 oz Mozzarella cheese, cut into 5 mm/¼ inch dice
50 g/2 oz cooked lean ham, cut into 5 mm/¼ inch dice (optional)
*dry white breadcrumbs for coating*
*oil for deep frying*

**American**

2 eggs
*cold risotto, made with 2 cups rice (see page 82)*
⅔ cup Mozzarella cheese, cut into ¼ inch dice
¼ cup processed ham, cut into ¼ inch dice (optional)
*dry white bread crumbs for coating*
*oil for deep frying*

Beat the eggs lightly. Stir them gently but thoroughly into the risotto, to bind. Put a rounded 15 ml spoon/1 tablespoon of risotto in the palm of one hand. Place 3 pieces of cheese, and 3 pieces of ham if used, in the centre and cover with another spoonful of risotto. Form into a ball so that the filling is completely enclosed. Roll each ball in breadcrumbs until thoroughly coated, then place in the refrigerator. Chill for 1 to 2 hours until the *supplì* are firm.

Heat the oil in a deep fryer to 190°C/375°F and fry 4 or 5 balls at a time, for about 5 minutes or until crisp and golden and the cheese inside has melted. Drain on crumpled kitchen paper towels and keep warm in the oven until all the rice balls are cooked. Serve hot.
SERVES 4 TO 6

# STRACCIATELLA

### 'Ragged' Egg Soup

A light and nourishing soup whose name derives from the 'little rags' formed by the egg. Use a well flavoured homemade chicken or meat stock as the basis for *Stracciatella*.

**Metric/Imperial**

1.2 litres/2 pints chicken or beef stock
2 eggs
2 × 15 ml spoons/2 tablespoons fine semolina
50 g/2 oz grated Parmesan cheese
1 × 15 ml spoon/1 tablespoon finely chopped fresh parsley
*pinch of grated nutmeg*
*salt*
*freshly ground black pepper*
TO SERVE:
*freshly grated Parmesan cheese*

**American**

5 cups chicken or beef stock
2 eggs
2 tablespoons semolina flour
¼ cup grated Parmesan cheese
1 tablespoon finely chopped fresh parsley
*pinch of grated nutmeg*
*salt*
*freshly ground black pepper*
TO SERVE:
*freshly grated Parmesan cheese*

Set aside 200 ml/⅓ pint/1 cup of the stock. Pour the remainder into a saucepan and bring it nearly to boiling point. Beat together the eggs, semolina, cheese, parsley and nutmeg, then stir in the reserved stock.

Whisk this mixture into the soup and continue heating gently just until the egg breaks up into flakes. Season to taste with salt and pepper and serve immediately in warmed soup bowls. Pass extra grated Parmesan separately. Serve with *grissini* or crusty bread.
SERVES 4 TO 6

# BUCATINI ALL' AMATRICIANA

### Pasta with Bacon, Pepper and Tomatoes

This favourite Roman dish takes its name from the little town of Amatrice in the Sabine hills. Originally made with *bucatini*, a small hollow macaroni, nowadays spaghetti is the pasta commonly used. Be sure to cook the pasta until just *al dente* and serve immediately.

**Metric/Imperial**

175 g/6 oz pickled streaky pork or unsmoked bacon
75 g/3 oz onion, finely chopped
1 small green chilli pepper, seeded and chopped
0.5 kg/1 lb tomatoes, skinned, seeded and chopped
350 g/12 oz bucatini or spaghetti
50 g/2 oz grated Pecorino or Parmesan cheese
*freshly ground black pepper*
*salt*

Stracciatella

## [Bucatini all' Amatriciana]

**American**

6 oz pickled salt pork or slab bacon
¾ cup finely chopped onion
1 small green chili pepper, seeded and chopped
1 lb tomatoes, skinned, seeded and chopped
¾ lb bucatini or spaghetti
¼ cup grated Pecorino or Parmesan cheese
freshly ground black pepper
salt

Cut the pork or bacon into thin strips, about 2½ cm/1 inch long. Cook in a heavy based saucepan very gently, without additional fat, until crisp and golden. Remove from the pan and keep hot.

In the fat remaining in the pan, fry the onion and pepper gently until beginning to soften. Add the tomatoes and cook rapidly for about 5 minutes until they are soft but retain their fresh taste.

Cook the pasta in plenty of fast boiling salted water for about 10 to 12 minutes, or until *al dente*. Drain thoroughly. Sprinkle the cheese into the bottom of a serving dish, add the hot pasta and toss together with two forks until the cheese has thoroughly melted.

Add the pork to the sauce, reheat and season with pepper, adding salt only if necessary. Pile the sauce in the centre of the spaghetti and serve immediately in deep plates.

SERVES 4

Pomodori col Riso, Bucatini all' Amatriciana

# POMODORI COL RISO

*Tomatoes stuffed with Rice*

Baked in a white lined oven-to-table dish, these tomatoes add a fine splash of colour to a plain roast meal. They may alternatively be served as a starter.

**Metric/Imperial**

6 large firm tomatoes
100 g/4 oz rice
2 cloves garlic, crushed
3 × 15 ml spoons/3 tablespoons olive oil (approximately)
1 × 15 ml spoon/1 tablespoon chopped fresh basil or 1 × 5 ml spoon/1 teaspoon dried basil
2 × 15 ml spoons/2 tablespoons water
salt
freshly ground black pepper
small parsley sprigs to garnish

**American**

6 large firm tomatoes
⅓ cup rice
2 cloves garlic, crushed
3 tablespoons olive oil (approximately)
1 tablespoon chopped fresh basil or 1 teaspoon dried basil
2 tablespoons water
salt
freshly ground black pepper
small parsley sprigs to garnish

Cut a slice off the top of each tomato. Using a teaspoon, scoop out the pulp into a basin, discarding the hard central core, but retaining the juice and seeds. Add the rice, garlic, oil, basil, water and generous seasonings of salt and pepper to the tomato pulp. Mix well.

Sprinkle the insides of the tomatoes with oil, season lightly with salt and arrange in an oiled ovenproof dish. Two-thirds fill each tomato with the filling mixture. Replace the 'lids' so that the rice is completely covered.

Cover the dish loosely with a lid or foil and cook in a moderate oven (180°C/350°F, Gas Mark 4) for about 1 hour.

Garnish each tomato with a sprig of parsley and serve hot with roast meat or poultry.

SERVES 6

*Lazio, Abruzzi & Molise*

# CANNELLONI

Cannelloni are oblong pieces of pasta, preferably homemade, filled and rolled like pancakes, topped with a sauce, then cooked and browned in the oven. Fillings can be made from fresh or cooked minced (ground) meat, cheese or from a light mixture of cheese and spinach.

## Metric/Imperial

FILLING:
2 × 15 ml spoons/2 tablespoons oil
50 g/2 oz onion, finely chopped
1 clove garlic, crushed
225 g/8 oz lean finely minced beef
2 tomatoes, skinned, seeded and chopped
1 × 15 ml spoon/1 tablespoon fine breadcrumbs
25 g/1 oz grated Parmesan cheese
1 × 5 ml spoon/1 teaspoon chopped fresh marjoram or ½ × 2.5 ml spoon/¼ teaspoon dried marjoram
1 egg, lightly beaten
salt
freshly ground black pepper

SAUCE:
40 g/1½ oz butter
40 g/1½ oz flour
300 ml/½ pint hot milk
150 ml/¼ pint hot single cream
salt
white pepper
grated nutmeg

PASTA:
8 pieces of wide lasagne or homemade pasta, each about 7.5 × 10 cm/3 × 4 inches (see page 58)

TOPPING:
25 g/1 oz grated Parmesan cheese
15 g/½ oz butter

## American

FILLING:
2 tablespoons oil
½ cup finely chopped onion
1 clove garlic, crushed
1 cup finely ground beef
2 tomatoes, skinned, seeded and chopped
1 tablespoon fine bread crumbs
¼ cup grated Parmesan cheese
1 teaspoon chopped fresh marjoram or ¼ teaspoon dried marjoram
1 egg, lightly beaten
salt
freshly ground black pepper

SAUCE:
3 tablespoons butter
⅓ cup flour
1¼ cups hot milk
⅔ cup hot light cream
salt
white pepper
grated nutmeg

PASTA:
8 pieces of wide lasagne or homemade pasta, each about 3 × 4 inches (see page 58)

TOPPING:
¼ cup grated Parmesan cheese
1 tablespoon butter

To prepare the filling, heat the oil in a saucepan, fry the onion and garlic very gently until soft but not coloured, add the minced (ground) meat and cook, stirring, until the meat changes colour. Add the tomatoes, cover and cook gently for 10 minutes. Take off the heat and stir in the breadcrumbs, cheese, marjoram, egg, salt and pepper. Leave to cool.

To make the sauce, melt the butter in a saucepan, add the flour and cook very gently for 1 minute. Remove from the heat, add the milk and cream all at once and beat with a wire whisk until smoothly mixed. Return to the heat and bring to the boil, whisking all the time. Season to taste with salt, pepper and nutmeg. Cover and keep warm.

To cook the pasta, bring a large pan of well salted water to the boil. Drop the pieces of pasta, several at a time, into the bubbling water. Stir for a moment to prevent them sticking to each other, and cook until just tender, about 5 minutes for homemade pasta, according to packet directions for manufactured pasta. Remove the pasta sheets with a slotted spoon, drain well, lay flat side by side on a clean cloth, and leave to cool a little.

Spoon a little of the filling down one long side of each piece of pasta and roll up. Arrange side by side in a well buttered ovenproof dish. Spoon the sauce over the pasta, making sure it is completely covered. Sprinkle with Parmesan cheese and dot with butter.

Bake, uncovered, in a preheated moderately hot oven (190°C/375°F, Gas Mark 5) for 20 to 30 minutes until bubbling hot and golden.

Serve with a crisp green salad and French bread.

SERVES 4

*Cannelloni (left); Piselli al Prosciutto (right)*

# SPAGHETTI ALLA CARBONARA

*Spaghetti with Egg and Bacon*

When making this popular pasta dish, it is very important that the eggs remain moist and creamy, so have all the other ingredients ready before you start to cook the eggs.

**Metric/Imperial**

350 g/12 oz spaghetti
175 g/6 oz streaky bacon rashers
3 eggs
2 × 15 ml spoons/2 tablespoons single cream
40 g/1½ oz grated Parmesan or Pecorino cheese
salt
freshly ground black pepper
40 g/1½ oz butter

**American**

¾ lb spaghetti
9 bacon slices
3 eggs
2 tablespoons light cream
6 tablespoons grated Parmesan or Pecorino cheese
salt
freshly ground black pepper
3 tablespoons butter

Lower the spaghetti into a large pan of fast boiling salted water and cook until tender but *al dente*, about 10 minutes. Drain thoroughly.

Cut the bacon into 1 cm/½ inch strips and fry gently in a dry frying pan (skillet) until crisp and golden. Beat the eggs with the cream, add the cheese and season lightly with salt but liberally with pepper.

When the spaghetti is ready, heat the butter in a large saucepan, add the egg mixture and stir over a moderate heat until just beginning to thicken. Immediately add the fried bacon and the spaghetti and toss lightly together. Serve at once.

SERVES 4

Spaghetti alla Carbonara

*Lazio, Abruzzi & Molise*

# PISELLI AL PROSCIUTTO

*Braised Peas with Prosciutto*

This favourite Italian way with young peas also makes a 'special' dish from frozen peas. For a less expensive version, use cooked (processed) ham or bacon instead of prosciutto. Serve as a course on their own, or with roast or grilled (broiled) meat or poultry.

**Metric/Imperial**

25 g/1 oz butter
50 g/2 oz onion, finely chopped
4 × 15 ml spoons/4 tablespoons chicken stock or water
275 g/10 oz shelled young peas, fresh or frozen and thawed
50 g/2 oz lean prosciutto or cooked ham, cut into small, thin strips
salt
freshly ground black pepper

**American**

2 tablespoons butter
½ cup finely chopped onion
¼ cup chicken stock or water
2 cups shelled young peas, fresh or frozen and thawed
¼ cup lean prosciutto or processed ham, cut into small, thin strips
salt
freshly ground black pepper

Melt the butter in a saucepan and sauté the onion very gently for 5 to 6 minutes until beginning to soften. Add the stock and peas, bring to the boil, cover and simmer for 5 minutes for frozen peas, 15 to 20 minutes for fresh peas.

Add the prosciutto or ham and cook, uncovered, stirring frequently, until the liquid is absorbed. Check the seasoning and serve hot.

SERVES 3 TO 4

41

*Lazio, Abruzzi & Molise*

# AGNELLO CON PEPERONI

*Lamb with Sweet Peppers*

You can make this dish with best end of neck lamb cutlets (lamb rib chops), or more economically with middle neck chops.

**Metric/Imperial**

1 kg/2 lb lamb (see above)
salt
freshly ground black pepper
flour for coating
2 × 15 ml spoons/2 tablespoons olive oil
2 cloves garlic, crushed
300 ml/½ pint dry white wine
6 peppers, mixed red and green if possible
4 tomatoes, skinned and quartered
1 bay leaf

**American**

2 lb lamb (see above)
salt
freshly ground black pepper
flour for dusting
2 tablespoons olive oil
2 cloves garlic, crushed
1¼ cups dry white wine
6 peppers, mixed green and red if possible
4 tomatoes, skinned and quartered
1 bay leaf

Trim excess fat from the meat, sprinkle with salt and pepper, and coat with flour, rubbing it into the meat.

Heat the olive oil and garlic in a large flameproof casserole, add the meat and fry until lightly browned, turning once or twice. Pour in the wine and allow to bubble briskly for a few minutes until reduced by one-third.

Cut the peppers into quarters and discard the pith and the seeds. Add the peppers, tomatoes and bay leaf to the lamb. Cover tightly and simmer very gently for 45 minutes or until the lamb is tender. Check the seasoning and serve from the casserole.

SERVES 4

# CODA ALLA VACCINARA

*Braised Oxtail with Celery*

For this dish, choose a meaty oxtail from a fairly young animal. The sauce reduces during the long slow cooking, but should there be any left use it to moisten a dish of pasta.

**Metric/Imperial**

1.25 kg/2½ lb oxtail, cut into 3.5 cm/1½ inch pieces
salt
freshly ground black pepper
flour for coating
3 × 15 ml spoons/3 tablespoons oil
1 small onion, finely chopped
2 cloves garlic, chopped
150 ml/¼ pint dry white or red wine
300 ml/½ pint beef stock
1 × 400 g/14 oz can peeled tomatoes
1 × 5 ml spoon/1 teaspoon tomato purée
1 sprig of thyme
1 bay leaf
3 cloves
1 celery heart, cut into 2.5 cm × 5 mm/
   1 × ¼ inch strips

**American**

2½ lb oxtail, cut into 1½ inch pieces
salt
freshly ground black pepper
flour for coating
3 tablespoons oil
1 small onion, finely chopped
2 cloves garlic, chopped
⅔ cup dry white or red wine
1¼ cups beef stock
1 × 14 oz can peeled tomatoes
1 teaspoon tomato paste
1 sprig of thyme
1 bay leaf
3 cloves
1 celery heart, cut into 1 × ¼ inch strips

Abbacchio Brodettato, Agnello con Peperoni, Maiale allo Spiedo

Season the oxtail with salt and pepper and then roll in flour until well coated. Heat the oil in a large flameproof casserole, add the oxtail and brown over fairly brisk heat, turning as necessary. Transfer the oxtail to a plate.

Lower the heat, add the onion and garlic to the pan and fry gently, stirring frequently, until beginning to turn golden. Return the oxtail, add the wine and heat briskly until the wine has reduced by half.

Stir in the stock, the tomatoes with their liquid, the tomato purée (paste), thyme, bay leaf and cloves. Bring to the boil, then transfer to the centre of a preheated cool oven (150°C/300°F, Gas Mark 2) and cook for at least 3 hours or until the oxtail is almost tender. Meanwhile cover the celery with boiling water, simmer for 10 minutes and drain.

Skim as much fat as possible from the surface of the oxtail sauce. Stir in the celery and cook for another 30 minutes or until tender. Check the seasoning before serving.

SERVES 4

Lazio, Abruzzi & Molise

# ABBACCHIO BRODETTATO

Baby Lamb in Egg and Lemon Sauce

Abbacchio is a lamb too young to have tasted grass, but this favourite Roman recipe is delicate and delicious made with a lean shoulder of young spring lamb.

**Metric/Imperial**
0.75 kg/1½ lb boneless shoulder of lamb
50 g/2 oz lean unsmoked bacon
25 g/1 oz lard
50 g/2 oz onion, chopped
2 × 15 ml spoons/2 tablespoons flour
salt
freshly ground black pepper
4 × 15 ml spoons/4 tablespoons white wine
450 ml/¾ pint stock or water
2 egg yolks
juice of ½ lemon
1 × 15 ml spoon/1 tablespoon chopped fresh parsley
1 × 5 ml spoon/1 teaspoon chopped fresh marjoram or ½ × 2.5 ml spoon/¼ teaspoon dried marjoram

**American**
1½ lb boneless shoulder of lamb
3 slices lean bacon
2 tablespoons lard
¼ cup chopped onion
2 tablespoons all-purpose flour
salt
freshly ground black pepper
¼ cup white wine
2 cups stock or water
2 egg yolks
juice of ½ lemon
1 tablespoon chopped fresh parsley
1 teaspoon chopped fresh marjoram or ¼ teaspoon dried marjoram

Cut the lamb into 2.5 cm/1 inch cubes and the bacon into 5 mm/¼ inch dice. Melt the lard in a saucepan and fry the bacon for a few minutes until the fat begins to run. Add the onion and lamb and fry, stirring frequently, until golden.

Sprinkle in the flour with salt and pepper to taste and cook, stirring, for 1 to 2 minutes. Add the wine and allow to bubble until almost completely evaporated, then stir in the stock or water and bring to the boil.

Cover tightly and simmer very gently for 45 minutes or until the meat is tender, stirring occasionally. Skim off any fat that may have risen to the surface.

Shortly before serving, beat together the egg yolks, lemon juice, parsley and marjoram and stir in 3 × 15 ml spoons/3 tablespoons of the hot lamb stock. Stir into the *brodettato* and cook over low heat, stirring constantly, until the egg has cooked and the sauce is thick enough to coat the back of a wooden spoon. Do not allow to boil or the sauce will curdle. Check the seasoning and serve at once.
SERVES 4

# MAIALE ALLO SPIEDO

Pork on a Skewer

**Metric/Imperial**
0.5 kg/1 lb fillet of pork
2–3 slices firm bread, 1 cm/½ inch thick
100 g/4 oz thinly sliced prosciutto or raw gammon
8 bay leaves, halved
salt
olive oil

**American**
1 lb pork tenderloin
2–3 slices firm bread, ½ inch thick
¼ lb thinly sliced prosciutto or raw smoked ham slice
8 bay leaves, halved
salt
freshly ground black pepper
olive oil

Cut the pork into 12 cubes.

Remove the crusts and cut the bread into 12 cubes of approximately the same size as the meat. Remove any rind and cut the prosciutto or gammon (smoked ham slice) into 12 pieces.

Divide the pork, prosciutto, bay leaves and bread equally between 4 kebab or long metal skewers, placing them on alternately. Lay the skewers flat, slightly apart, in a well oiled baking tin. Sprinkle lightly with salt, generously with pepper, and then liberally with oil.

Bake in the centre of a preheated moderately hot oven (190°C/375°F, Gas Mark 5) for 30 to 40 minutes until the meat is cooked and the bread crisp and crunchy. Turn the skewers once half-way through cooking.

Serve hot. Stuffed tomatoes or mushrooms go well with this dish.
SERVES 4

# Tuscany, Umbria & The Marches

Both geographically and historically the ancient region of Tuscany lies at the very heart of Italy. To the North and East the region is encircled by the Appenine Mountains, from whence it sweeps through hill country indented by fertile river valleys down to a long coastal plain bordering the Tyrrhenian Sea. The Tuscans themselves are descendants of the Etruscans, from whom they have inherited an independent spirit and a robust love of life and good food. Luckily for them their needs are well catered for, as the land, rivers and sea of Tuscany provide some of the best wine and food in Italy.

Change has been slow in reaching this area and much of the cuisine retains its original simplicity and robustness. Tuscan recipes have developed around the local produce. The Chiana valley and its renowned beef cattle produce the famous Florentine steaks. In the hill country, pigs are reared in vast numbers to provide the excellent pork, ham, salami and sausages. Chicken are plentiful, and Tuscan ways of cooking them are original. A visit to any of the local markets will confirm the variety and quality of the fresh vegetables, fruits and herbs. Fresh herbs are a feature of Tuscan cooking, especially rosemary, sage and fennel. Spinach is combined with curd cheese and Parmesan to make excellent green *gnocchi* (see page 52), and the same mixture is used as a filling for cannelloni or ravioli. But the vegetable of Tuscany is undoubtedly a small white bean, similar to a haricot (navy) bean but used fresh rather than dried. These white beans appear in thick vegetable soups, with tuna fish and on their own. So fond are the Tuscans of their native beans that they are sometimes called 'the bean eaters' by their fellow countrymen.

The neighbouring regions of Umbria and the Marches have many food traditions in common with Tuscany and with each other, yet both have regional specialities of their own based on local produce. With its long coastline bordering the Adriatic, The Marches takes pride in its fish stews and soup, and the *brodetto* of Ancona is famous. Umbria, straddling the Appenines with Perugia and Assisi at its heart, bases its cuisine on pork, lamb, veal and small game, together with fish from Lake Trasimeno. A rare Umbrian treat are the black truffles from Norcia. Also from Norcia comes the renowned *porchetta* (roast sucking pigs) and the products of the pig such as salami, sausages and smoked hams. In Umbria, as well as in Tuscany, roast loin of pork flavoured with rosemary is popular for important family occasions, yet the women are also adept at making robust and tasty dishes from inexpensive ingredients such as tripe. Excellent fish are caught along the coast and Leghorn is renowned for *cacciucco*, an unusually spicy fish stew.

Both Tuscany and Umbria are famous for their wines. The great wine of Tuscany is, of course, red Chianti, the very best of which comes from the small *Chianti Classico* area lying between Florence and Sienna. Young, fruity red Chianti is perfect with pasta dishes, while with age it matures into a full-bodied wine ideal for serving with roasts. The great wine of Umbria is Orvieto, available *secco* (dry) or *abboccato* (medium).

45

# RIBOLLITA

*Thick Bean and Vegetable Soup*

This hearty Tuscan soup takes some time to prepare, so it is frequently made in large quantities and reheated next day. It is distinguished from other vegetable soups by the addition of a little olive oil immediately before serving.

**Metric/Imperial**
225 g/8 oz haricot beans, soaked in water overnight
5 × 15 ml spoons/5 tablespoons olive oil
1 onion, chopped
1 clove garlic, crushed
1 stick celery, chopped
2 leeks, thinly sliced
0.5 kg/1 lb green cabbage, finely shredded
1 sprig each of thyme and rosemary, tied together
1 × 15 ml spoon/1 tablespoon tomato purée
salt
freshly ground black pepper
2 × 15 ml spoons/2 tablespoons chopped fresh parsley
TO SERVE:
1 large slice bread, cut into 3 mm/⅛ inch dice and lightly browned in the oven

Carciofi Ripieni

**American**
1 cup plus 2 tablespoons navy beans, soaked in water overnight
⅓ cup olive oil
1 onion, chopped
1 clove garlic, crushed
1 stalk celery, chopped
2 leeks, thinly sliced
6 cups finely shredded green cabbage
1 sprig of thyme and rosemary, tied together
1 tablespoon tomato paste
salt
freshly ground black pepper
2 tablespoons chopped fresh parsley
TO SERVE:
1 large slice bread, cut into ⅛ inch dice and lightly browned in the oven

Drain the beans and place in a saucepan. Add 1.75 litres/3 pints/7½ cups cold water, bring to the boil, cover, and simmer for about 3 hours or until tender.

When the beans are nearly cooked, heat 3 × 15 ml spoons/3 tablespoons of the oil in a large saucepan, add the onion, garlic and celery and fry gently for 10 minutes, stirring frequently. Add the leeks, cabbage and herbs and stir for 3 to 4 minutes.

Drain the beans and add the cooking liquor to the vegetables together with the tomato purée (paste) and salt and pepper to taste. Bring to the boil and simmer for about 30 minutes. Add the beans, with

more water as necessary, and continue simmering until all the vegetables are tender.

Remove the herbs, check the seasoning, and immediately before serving stir in the remaining oil and the parsley. Serve boiling hot and hand the bread dice separately. Grated cheese can be served with this soup if wished.
SERVES 6 TO 8

# CARCIOFI RIPIENI

*Stuffed Artichokes*

**Metric/Imperial**
4 large globe artichokes
25 g/1 oz butter
3 × 15 ml spoons/3 tablespoons oil
½ small onion, finely chopped
1 clove garlic, crushed
4 mushrooms, sliced
few small cauliflower florets
2 × 15 ml spoons/2 tablespoons white breadcrumbs
1 × 15 ml spoon/1 tablespoon chopped fresh parsley
salt
freshly ground black pepper
6 × 15 ml spoons/6 tablespoons dry white wine
parsley sprigs to garnish

**American**
4 large globe artichokes
2 tablespoons butter
3 tablespoons oil
½ small onion, finely chopped
1 clove garlic, crushed
4 mushrooms, sliced
few small cauliflower florets
2 tablespoons white bread crumbs
1 tablespoon chopped fresh parsley
salt
freshly ground black pepper
6 tablespoons dry white wine
parsley sprigs to garnish

Cut off the stalks and trim the bases of the artichokes so that they stand upright. Pull off the coarse outer leaves and cut off the top third of the remaining leaves which are inedible. Pull the leaves back and remove the hairy 'choke' in the centre.

Heat the butter and 1 × 15 ml spoon/1 tablespoon oil in a small saucepan, add the onion, garlic, mushrooms and cauliflower and fry gently for 5 minutes, stirring frequently. Stir in the breadcrumbs, parsley and salt and pepper to taste. Fill artichokes with this mixture.

Heat the rest of the oil in a large pan. Stand the artichokes side by side in the pan. Add the wine, cover tightly and simmer over a very low heat for 40 minutes to 1 hour, until tender. Garnish with parsley sprigs before serving.
SERVES 4

# TORTINO DI CARCIOFI

*Baked Artichoke Omelet*

The artichokes for this dish must be very small, young and tender like those used in Tuscany. Although they do not have quite the same flavour, canned or frozen artichoke hearts can be used instead.

**Metric/Imperial**
8 small artichokes or canned artichoke hearts, well drained, or frozen artichoke hearts, defrosted
flour for dusting
2 × 15 ml spoons/2 tablespoons olive oil
6 eggs
salt
*freshly ground black pepper*

**American**
8 small artichokes or canned artichoke hearts, well drained, or frozen artichoke hearts, defrosted
all-purpose flour for dusting
2 tablespoons olive oil
6 eggs
salt
*freshly ground black pepper*

Butter a shallow 23 cm/9 inch diameter baking dish, or 4 individual dishes, and put into the oven, set at moderately hot (200°C/400°F, Gas Mark 6), to heat.

Discard the tough outer leaves and stalks from the artichokes, trim the tips of the leaves and cut into quarters. Remove the inner piece of 'choke' from each quarter. (If using canned or frozen artichokes simply cut into quarters.) Dust the

pieces of artichoke lightly with flour. Heat the oil in a frying pan (skillet) and fry the artichokes over a moderate heat, stirring frequently, for 5 minutes or until golden brown.

Break the eggs into a basin, season with salt and pepper and beat until slightly frothy. Spread the drained artichokes in the base of the preheated dish, pour over the eggs and bake in the top of the oven for 10 minutes or until lightly set.

Place under a preheated grill (broiler) for a few seconds to brown and crisp the surface. Cut into wedges and serve immediately.
SERVES 4

Ribollita

*Tuscany, Umbria & The Marches*

## CROSTINI ALLA FIORENTINA

*Chicken Liver Toasts*

These small savouries are equally good served as an antipasto or as light snacks. Unless you are accustomed to it, sage flavouring needs to be used sparingly.

**Metric/Imperial**

225 g/8 oz chicken livers
40 g/1½ oz butter
1 small shallot, finely chopped
3–4 fresh sage leaves
freshly ground black pepper
8 pieces bread, 5 mm/¼ inch thick (either triangles cut from a small sandwich loaf or oval slices from a French loaf)
butter for shallow frying
squeeze of lemon juice
1 × 15 ml spoon/1 tablespoon chopped fresh parsley

**American**

½ lb chicken livers
3 tablespoons butter
1 small shallot, finely chopped
3–4 fresh sage leaves
freshly ground black pepper
8 pieces bread, ¼ inch thick (either triangles cut from a small sandwich loaf or oval slices from a French loaf)
butter for shallow frying
squeeze of lemon juice
1 tablespoon chopped fresh parsley

Crostini alla Fiorentina

Wash the livers and cut away any tissues or discoloured parts, then chop finely. Melt the butter in a small saucepan and gently sauté the shallot and sage leaves together for about 5 minutes. Discard the sage leaves.

Add the livers and a few grinds of pepper and cook gently, stirring frequently, until the livers are no longer pink, about 6 minutes. Meanwhile, fry the bread croûtes in butter until crisp and golden on each side; drain on kitchen paper towels. Stir the lemon juice into the liver mixture, check the seasoning, spread over the croûtes and sprinkle with parsley. Serve immediately.

SERVES 4

## FAGIOLI TOSCANI COL TONNO

*Beans with Tuna Fish*

In Tuscany this robust antipasto is made with fresh white beans, best quality canned tuna fish and good olive oil.

**Metric/Imperial**

175 g/6 oz dried haricot beans, soaked in water overnight
1 small onion, thinly sliced
olive oil for dressing
salt
freshly ground black pepper
1 × 225 g/8 oz can tuna fish
chopped fresh parsley to garnish

**American**

1 cup less 2 tablespoons dried navy beans, soaked in water overnight
1 small onion, thinly sliced
olive oil for dressing
salt
freshly ground black pepper
1 × 8 oz can tuna fish
chopped fresh parsley to garnish

Drain the beans, place in a saucepan and cover with fresh cold water. Bring to the boil, cover and simmer for 2½ to 3 hours, until tender. Drain and while still hot mix with the onion, a liberal dressing of olive oil, and salt and pepper to taste.

When cold, put into bowls, add tuna fish and sprinkle with parsley.

SERVES 3 TO 4

## FINOCCHIO ALLA FIORENTINA

*Fennel with Butter and Cheese*

Bulbs of Florentine fennel provide a gentle anise-flavoured vegetable which is delicious served alone, or with meat.

**Metric/Imperial**

4 medium bulbs fennel
1 × 15 ml spoon/1 tablespoon olive oil
1 clove garlic
1 slice of lemon
1 × 5 ml spoon/1 teaspoon salt
25 g/1 oz butter
2 × 15 ml spoons/2 tablespoons grated Parmesan cheese
freshly ground black pepper

**American**

4 medium bulbs fennel
1 tablespoon olive oil
1 clove garlic
1 slice of lemon
1 teaspoon salt
2 tablespoons butter
2 tablespoons grated Parmesan cheese
freshly ground black pepper

Trim the top shoots and bases of the fennel bulbs, and use a potato peeler to peel off any discoloured parts. Wash in cold water. Cut into segments.

Put into a saucepan containing enough boiling water to cover the fennel. Add the oil, garlic, lemon and salt. Bring to the boil, cover and simmer for 20 minutes or until just tender.

Melt the butter in a shallow gratin dish. Drain the fennel well, put into the dish and turn gently to coat with butter. Sprinkle with cheese and pepper. Brown lightly under the grill (broiler) before serving.

SERVES 4

Fagioli Toscani col Tonno, Finocchio alla Fiorentina (right)

# TRIGLIE ALLA MARINARA

*Grilled (Broiled) Red Mullet (Snapper)*

These beautiful fish are plentiful off the coast of Tuscany and this simple grilled (broiled) recipe is one of the best ways of cooking them. Any small round fish can be cooked in the same manner, either under the grill (broiler) or, better still, outdoors over a barbecue in true sailor fashion.

**Metric/Imperial**
4 red mullet, about 225 g/8 oz each
3 × 15 ml spoons/3 tablespoons olive oil
1 × 5 ml spoon/1 teaspoon salt
freshly ground black pepper
4 cloves garlic, sliced
25 g/1 oz dried white breadcrumbs
lemon wedges to garnish

**American**
2 red snapper, about 1 lb each
3 tablespoons olive oil
1 teaspoon salt
freshly ground black pepper
4 cloves garlic, sliced
¼ cup dried white bread crumbs
lemon wedges to garnish

Ask the fishmonger to clean the mullet but leave the heads on. Put the oil, salt and a seasoning of pepper in a shallow dish, add the fish and leave to marinate for at least 1 hour, turning once.

Drain the fish, reserving the marinade and put a little garlic inside each fish. Grill (broil) under a moderate heat for 6 to 8 minutes each side, turning the fish once.

About 3 minutes before the cooking is completed, sprinkle the fish with breadcrumbs, spoon over some of the reserved marinade to moisten, and complete the cooking. Serve hot, garnished with lemon wedges.

SERVES 4

# POLLO AL MATTONE

*Tuscan Pressed Chicken*

There is no real translation for this unique Tuscan way of cooking chicken. A 'mattone' is a round terracotta cooking platter with an exceedingly heavy lid. You can get a fairly similar result by using a heavy based frying pan (skillet) together with a flat lid which fits inside the pan and can be weighted down to press the chicken. Instead of rosemary and bay leaf, Tuscan cooks often put 3 or 4 fresh sage leaves on the chicken while it cooks.

**Metric/Imperial**
1 small chicken, about 1 kg/2 lb
3 × 15 ml spoons/3 tablespoons olive oil
1 large clove garlic, crushed
1 bay leaf, crumbled
1 sprig of rosemary
1 × 5 ml spoon/1 teaspoon salt
freshly ground black pepper
juice of ½ lemon

**American**
1 small chicken, about 2 lb
3 tablespoons olive oil
1 large clove garlic, crushed
1 bay leaf, crumbled
1 sprig of rosemary
1 teaspoon salt
freshly ground black pepper
juice of ½ lemon

Cut the chicken in half along the backbone. Remove the backbone and beat the chicken as flat as possible. Wash and dry the 2 halves and place flat in a shallow dish. Mix all the remaining ingredients, except the lemon juice, together and pour over the chicken. Leave to marinate for 2 to 3 hours, turning once.

Oil the base of the mattone or frying pan (skillet) and heat gently. Put in the chicken and press the heavy lid down on top of it. Cook over a low to moderate heat for 30 to 40 minutes, until the chicken is golden brown and tender.

Sprinkle the lemon juice over the chicken and serve hot accompanied by a crisp green salad, or a spinach purée with any juices from the chicken poured over it.

SERVES 2

# BRACIOLE DI MAIALE UBRIACO

*Pork Chops in Wine*

A popular dish in Tuscany where the wine used is naturally, a young Chianti.

**Metric/Imperial**

4 lean pork chops, about 2 cm/¾ inch thick
salt
freshly ground black pepper
2 × 15 ml spoons/2 tablespoons olive oil
2 cloves garlic, crushed
2 × 15 ml spoons/2 tablespoons chopped fresh parsley
200 ml/⅓ pint light dry wine

**American**

4 lean pork chops, about ¾ inch thick
salt
freshly ground black pepper
2 tablespoons olive oil
2 cloves garlic, crushed
2 tablespoons chopped fresh parsley
1 cup light dry wine

Wash, trim and dry the chops and season with salt and pepper. Heat the oil in a large, shallow pan and fry the chops, uncovered, in a single layer for 3 to 4 minutes on each side, until lightly browned. Lift out on to a plate.

Add the garlic and parsley to the pan, stir and fry for 1 to 2 minutes, then pour in the wine and bring to simmering point. Return the chops to the pan, cover and simmer gently for 30 to 35 minutes, until tender.

Arrange the chops on a hot serving dish. Boil the pan juices rapidly, uncovered, until reduced by about half and spoon over the chops. Serve with creamed potatoes or plain rice, if liked. Traditionally, this dish is accompanied by a glass of young Chianti.
SERVES 4

# COLOMBI SELVATICI COI PISELLI

*Wood Pigeons with Peas*

Although Tuscans often cook small whole birds complete with their insides, for this recipe you need young, plump pigeons dressed and ready for cooking. Unless the pigeons are large, allow one per serving.

**Metric/Imperial**

4 young pigeons
salt
freshly ground black pepper
25 g/1 oz butter
2 × 15 ml spoons/2 tablespoons oil
450 g/1 lb shelled green peas
1 × 5 ml spoon/1 teaspoon sugar

**American**

4 young pigeons
salt
freshly ground black pepper
2 tablespoons butter
2 tablespoons oil
1 medium onion, chopped
5 bacon slices, derinded and diced
¾ cup dry white wine
1¼ cups chicken stock
3 cups shelled green peas
1 teaspoon sugar

Wash and dry the pigeons. Season inside and outside with salt and pepper.

In a large flameproof casserole, heat the butter and oil and fry the onion and bacon gently until the onion is soft and golden. Increase the heat, add the pigeons and cook, turning frequently, until golden brown all over, about 15 minutes.

Add the wine and allow to bubble briskly until reduced to half the quantity. Add the stock, bring to the boil, cover tightly and simmer very gently for 1¼ to 1½ hours, or until the pigeons are almost tender. Check the pan from time to time to make sure there is enough liquid, adding more stock if necessary.

Stir in the peas with the sugar and a little salt, cover and simmer gently for another 20 minutes, or until the peas and pigeons are tender.
SERVES 4

*150 ml/¼ pint dry white wine
300 ml/½ pint chicken stock
450 g/1 lb shelled green peas
1 × 5 ml spoon/1 teaspoon sugar*

*25 g/1 oz butter
2 × 15 ml spoons/2 tablespoons oil
1 medium onion, chopped
75 g/3 oz streaky bacon, derinded and diced*

Pollo al Mattone, Colombi Selvatici coi Piselli (left); Braciole di Maiale Ubriaco (below)

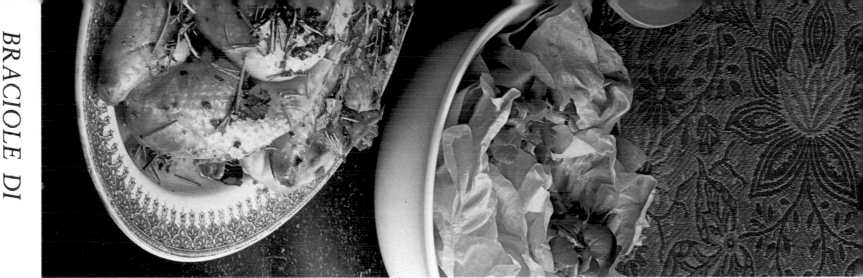

# LINGUA IN SALSA AGRODOLCE

### Tongue in Sweet-Sour Sauce

The Italian tradition of serving food in sweet-sour sauces is a survival from Roman times and is particularly good for rich or lightly salted meats. The tongue can be cooked in advance, or bought cooked and simply reheated in the sauce.

**Metric/Imperial**
1 lightly pickled ox tongue, about
  1.25 kg/2½ lb
1 large onion, sliced
2 carrots, grated
2 sticks celery, sliced
12 peppercorns
1 bay leaf
sprig of thyme
SAUCE:
3 × 15 ml spoons/3 tablespoons oil
1 medium onion, finely chopped
50 g/2 oz flour
900 ml/1½ pints hot beef stock
2 × 15 ml spoons/2 tablespoons
  redcurrant jelly
4 × 15 ml spoons/4 tablespoons red
  wine vinegar
50 g/2 oz brown sugar
2 × 15 ml spoons/2 tablespoons
  sultanas
2 × 15 ml spoons/2 tablespoons pine
  nuts or blanched slivered almonds
finely grated rind of 1 large orange
large pinch of ground cloves

**American**
1 lightly pickled ox tongue, about 2½ lb
1 large onion, sliced
2 carrots, grated
2 stalks celery, sliced
12 peppercorns
1 bay leaf
sprig of thyme
SAUCE:
3 tablespoons oil
1 medium onion, finely chopped
½ cup all-purpose flour
3¾ cups hot beef stock
2 tablespoons redcurrant jelly
¼ cup red wine vinegar
¼ cup brown sugar
2 tablespoons seedless white raisins
2 tablespoons pine nuts or blanched
  slivered almonds
finely grated rind of 1 large orange
large pinch of ground cloves

Soak the tongue in cold water for several hours. Drain, put into a saucepan, cover with cold water and bring slowly to the boil. Drain thoroughly, replace the tongue in the pan and cover with fresh cold water.

Add the onion, carrots, celery, peppercorns, bay leaf and thyme, cover tightly and simmer very gently for 3½ hours, or

Lingua in Salsa Agrodolce, Gnocchi Verdi

# GNOCCHI VERDI

Among the lightest and best of Italian gnocchi, these attractive green gnocchi can be prepared in advance. In Tuscany they are found under the name ravioli, and sometimes in cork shapes.

**Metric/Imperial**
0.5 kg/1 lb fresh spinach
salt
225 g/8 oz Ricotta or curd cheese
freshly ground black pepper
grated nutmeg
15 g/½ oz butter
2 eggs, lightly beaten
40 g/1½ oz grated Parmesan cheese
50 g/2 oz plain flour
TO SERVE:
50 g/2 oz butter
25 g/1 oz grated Parmesan cheese

**American**
1 lb fresh spinach
salt
½ lb Ricotta or curd cheese
freshly ground black pepper
grated nutmeg
1 tablespoon butter
2 eggs, lightly beaten
6 tablespoons grated Parmesan cheese
½ cup all-purpose flour
TO SERVE:
¼ cup butter
¼ cup grated Parmesan cheese

Remove the white stalks from the spinach. Put the cleaned leaves into a saucepan with a sprinkling of salt. Cover tightly and cook, without added water, for 10 to 15 minutes, or until tender. Drain well, then squeeze absolutely dry and chop very finely.

Return to the saucepan, add the Ricotta or curd cheese, salt, pepper and nutmeg, and the butter. Stir together over a very low heat for 3 to 4 minutes until evenly mixed and dry. Remove from the heat, beat in the eggs, Parmesan cheese and flour, mixing thoroughly. Set aside in a cool place until firm.

Take a heaped 15 ml spoon/tablespoon-ful of mixture at a time, and with well floured hands roll into a ball.

Lower the balls, a few at a time, into a pan of gently simmering salted water. When they rise to the top of the water, after 4 to 5 minutes, lift out with a slotted spoon and drain on kitchen paper towels. Transfer to a well buttered shallow oven-proof dish and keep hot in a warm oven.

When all are cooked, heat the butter until it begins to turn nut brown, pour over the gnocchi and sprinkle with Parmesan. Serve at once or leave in the oven for up to 5 minutes before serving.
SERVES 4

52

until the tongue is tender when pierced. Leave in the water for 30 minutes then drain, peel off the skin and trim the root end if necessary.

Meanwhile, prepare the sauce. Heat the oil in a saucepan and fry the onion gently until beginning to soften. Add the flour and cook, stirring, over a low heat until beginning to turn brown. Add the stock all at once and the redcurrant jelly. Heat, stirring constantly, until the sauce is smooth and boiling. Stir in the remaining ingredients, cover and simmer gently for 30 minutes.

Carve the tongue into thick slices, arrange them overlapping in a shallow ovenproof dish and pour the sauce over the meat. Cover and place in a preheated moderate oven (160°C/325°F, Gas Mark 3) for about 30 minutes, so that the meat becomes impregnated with the sauce and hot through.
SERVES 6 TO 8

# PANFORTE DI SIENA

*Siena Cake*

This flat 'cake' with a nougat-like texture, rich with candied peel, toasted nuts and spices, is a particular speciality of the town of Siena.

**Metric/Imperial**
75 g/3 oz hazelnuts
75 g/3 oz blanched almonds, coarsely chopped
175 g/6 oz candied peel, finely chopped
25 g/1 oz cocoa powder
50 g/2 oz plain flour
1 × 2.5 ml spoon/½ teaspoon ground cinnamon
½ × 2.5 ml spoon/¼ teaspoon mixed spice
100 g/4 oz caster sugar
100 g/4 oz honey
TOPPING:
2 × 15 ml spoons/2 tablespoons icing sugar
1 × 5 ml spoon/1 teaspoon ground cinnamon

**American**
½ cup filberts
½ cup coarsely chopped blanched almonds
1 cup finely chopped candied peel
¼ cup unsweetened cocoa powder
½ cup all-purpose flour
½ teaspoon ground cinnamon
¼ teaspoon mixed spice
½ cup sugar
⅓ cup honey
TOPPING:
2 tablespoons confectioners' sugar
1 teaspoon ground cinnamon

Spread the hazelnuts (filberts) on a baking sheet and put into a preheated moderately hot oven (190°C/375°F, Gas Mark 5) for 5 to 10 minutes, until the skins split and the nuts are lightly toasted. When cool enough to handle, rub the brown skins off in a rough cloth and chop the nuts coarsely. Put the hazelnuts (filberts), almonds, candied peel, cocoa, flour, cinnamon and spice into a mixing bowl and stir well.

Put the sugar and honey into a small saucepan, heat slowly until the sugar dissolves, then boil gently until a sugar thermometer registers 115°C/240°F, or until a little of the mixture dropped into a cup of cold water forms a soft ball. Take

*Panforte di Siena*

off the heat immediately, add the nut mixture and stir until well mixed.

Turn into a 20 cm/8 inch flan ring (pie pan) lined with well buttered greaseproof paper or non-stick parchment. Spread flat, making sure the mixture is no more than 1 cm/½ inch thick. Bake in a preheated cool oven (150°C/300°F, Gas Mark 2) for 30 to 35 minutes.

Allow to cool, then peel off the paper and sprinkle the top thickly with the icing (confectioners') sugar sifted with the cinnamon. Serve cut into small wedges.
MAKES 8 TO 12 PIECES

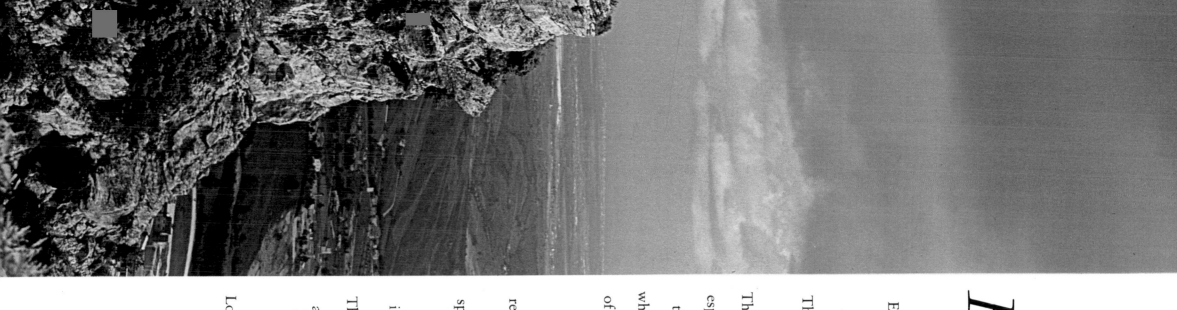

# Emilia-Romagna

Emilia-Romagna spans the top of the 'leg' of Italy, stretching from Liguria in the west to its popular seaside resorts along the Adriatic. It is among the most fertile areas of Italy, producing great quantities of vegetables, fruit, wheat and grapes. The region abounds in gastronomic specialities and is a mecca for anyone interested in good food. The people of Emilia-Romagna are considered to be the best trenchermen in Italy, and they undoubtedly have a great love of life as well as of cooking and eating.

The capital of the region is the ancient university town of Bologna, where the delicatessen and food shops have attention riveting displays of food, especially of pork products and cheeses. It is also difficult to choose between the many excellent restaurants there. I remain eternally grateful to the Bolognese who patiently taught me how to make their superlative egg pasta and to turn it into tortellini, the little coils of stuffed pasta which are a Christmas speciality. Legend has it that tortellini was invented by a lovelorn Bolognese chef inspired by a glimpse through the keyhole of his loved one's navel. A touching story, complicated by the fact that other towns of the region have other legends and claim the 'best' recipe!

The basic egg pasta cut into narrow ribbons becomes tagliatelle, Bologna's favourite pasta, or, cut into rectangles, it becomes lasagne.

The delightful market town of Parma in the centre of the district is renowned for the most famous pork speciality of the whole area, *prosciutto di Parma*, the sweet, tender, pale red ham, at its best when sliced wafer thin and eaten raw with melon or ripe figs. Other pork specialities are *zampone* (minced and seasoned pork stuffed into the foreleg of a pig) and *cotechino* (the same stuffing in a large sausage casing).

Both these products originated in Modena and both can be bought, nowadays in pre-cooked form, at delicatessens specializing in Italian foods. Other famous pork products include the large and rather bland Mortadella sausage and the delicate salami of Felino.

The area between Parma and Modena produces, and ages, Parmesan cheese. Eaten fresh, Parmesan has a delightfully piquant flavour, but, after ageing for 2 to 3 years, it becomes the cheese for cooking. Well-aged Parmesan can be grated finely, and quite small amounts have the unique ability of enhancing the flavour of any food with which it is combined. Parmesan, however, loses flavour after grating, so whenever possible buy it in a piece and grate it freshly as required. Loosely wrapped in polythene (plastic) it usually keeps well in a refrigerator.

When in Ravenna Marina or the coastal towns such as Rimini or Riccioni don't fail to visit the harbour side restaurants to sample the *brodetto* (fish stew made from the local catch) or the fish and shellfish impaled on sticks and barbecued while you wait.

Although not a famed wine region vast quantities of light red and white wines are produced and consumed in the area. The rather odd dry, semi-sparkling Lambrusco wines are worth mentioning because they are much recommended by the locals for counteracting the richness of the region's pork and pasta dishes.

# PROSCIUTTO CON MELONE

*Parma Ham with Melon*

There is just no substitute for the delicate flavour of raw smoked Parma ham. It is always served in paper thin slices and combines exquisitely with the sweetness of a ripe cantaloupe melon. It is also excellent served with fresh ripe figs.

**Metric/Imperial**
1 ripe melon
6–8 thin slices Parma ham

**American**
1 ripe melon
6–8 thin slices Parma ham

Chill, deseed and cut the melon into 6 to 8 slices. Serve each portion of melon with a slice of ham draped over it.
SERVES 6 TO 8

# CARCIOFI IN SALSA

*Dressed Artichoke Hearts*

In Italy small, tender, freshly cooked globe artichoke hearts are used for this dish, but canned artichoke hearts also make an excellent and quickly prepared antipasto.

**Metric/Imperial**
4 × 15 ml spoons/4 tablespoons olive oil
1 × 15 ml spoon/1 tablespoon lemon juice
2 × 5 ml spoons/2 teaspoons finely grated onion
1 small bay leaf
salt
freshly ground black pepper
16 small fresh, cooked, or canned artichoke hearts, drained
1 × 15 ml spoon/1 tablespoon chopped fresh parsley

**American**
¼ cup olive oil
1 tablespoon lemon juice
2 teaspoons finely grated onion
1 small bay leaf
salt
freshly ground black pepper
16 small fresh, cooked, or canned artichoke hearts, drained
1 tablespoon chopped fresh parsley

In a large bowl, mix together the olive oil, lemon juice, grated onion, bay leaf and salt and pepper to taste. Add the artichoke hearts, toss lightly and chill for 1 to 2 hours, stirring occasionally.

Arrange the artichokes in individual dishes and spoon over the dressing. Sprinkle with chopped parsley to garnish.
SERVES 4

# PASSATELLI IN BRODO ALL' EMILIANA

*Cheese Noodles in Broth*

Emilians use a *passatelli* for making these noodles, but a metal colander with spaghetti size holes can be used instead.

**Metric/Imperial**
1.2 litres/2 pints chicken or meat broth
25 g/1 oz fine dried white breadcrumbs
25 g/1 oz grated Parmesan cheese
2 × 5 ml spoons/2 teaspoons flour
1 small egg, beaten
15 g/½ oz butter, softened
salt
freshly ground black pepper
pinch of grated nutmeg
chopped fresh parsley to garnish

**American**
5 cups chicken or meat broth
¼ cup fine dried white bread crumbs
¼ cup grated Parmesan cheese
2 teaspoons flour
1 egg, beaten
1 tablespoon butter, softened
salt
freshly ground black pepper
pinch of grated nutmeg
chopped fresh parsley to garnish

Bring the broth to the boil in a wide saucepan. Put the breadcrumbs, cheese, flour, egg, butter, salt, pepper and nutmeg into a basin and work to a paste.

Press the paste through the holes of the colander directly into the boiling soup. Simmer for about 2 minutes until the noodles rise to the surface. Add parsley.
SERVES 4

Prosciutto con Melone (left); Passatelli in Brodo all' Emiliana, Carciofi in Salsa (right)

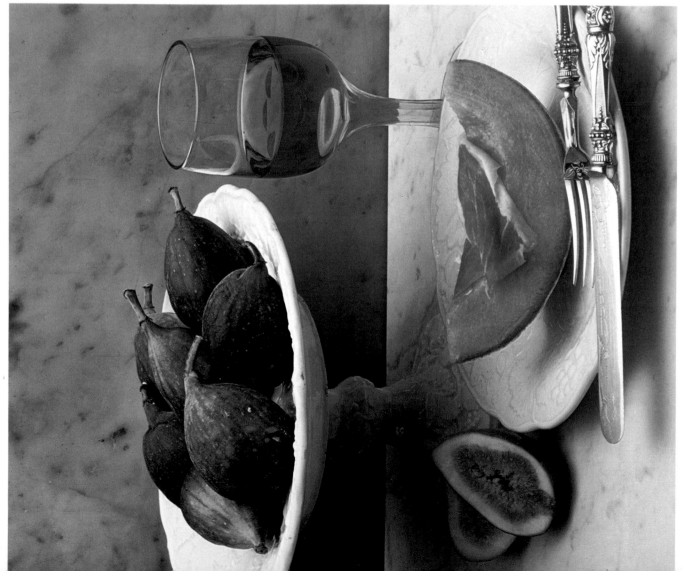

# PASTA ALL' UOVO

*Flat Egg Pasta*

This is the basic recipe for making the flat pasta common throughout Northern Italy. Made in small quantities it is easy to handle and can be cut into any of the flat pasta shapes or used for stuffed pastas.

**Metric/Imperial**
225 g/8 oz plain flour
2 large eggs
2 × 5 ml spoons/2 teaspoons oil
1 × 2.5 ml spoon/½ teaspoon salt
few drops of water (as necessary)

**American**
2 cups all-purpose flour
2 eggs
2 teaspoons oil
¼ teaspoon salt
few drops of water (as necessary)

Sift the flour into a heap on a working surface and make a wide hole in the centre. Crack the eggs into the hole, add the oil and salt and mix together with the finger-tips. Then gradually fold the flour over the egg mixture and knead with the hands until a crumbly dough is formed. Knead the crumbs together to form a stiff paste, adding a few drops of water where the mixture seems dry.

Dust the working surface and your hands lightly with flour and knead the dough strongly for 8 to 10 minutes until it becomes smooth and elastic. Wrap the dough in cling film (saran wrap) and set aside for about 1 hour.

Roll out the dough on a lightly floured surface, first in one direction and then the other, until it is paper thin. Dust the pasta lightly with flour and leave to rest for 10 to 20 minutes, so that it dries a little and becomes less inclined to stick. It is then ready to be cut into the required shapes.
MAKES ABOUT 350 G/12 OZ PASTA

*Pasta verde:*
Homemade *pasta verde* is an attractive pale green colour flecked with darker green. Use the basic recipe above, but, with the eggs, add 50 g/2 oz/¼ cup cooked spinach, squeezed very dry and either sieved or chopped very finely. Work into a paste, roll, cut and use as above. Green pasta tends to be stickier than plain pasta so it is necessary to flour the working surface more frequently.
MAKES ABOUT 400 G/14 OZ PASTA

*For taliarini, tagliatelle or fettuccine:*
Roll the sheet of pasta loosely into a Swiss (jelly) roll, and with a sharp knife cut it across into even strips 3 mm/⅛ inch wide for taliarini, 5 mm/¼ inch wide for tagliatelle or fettuccine. Shake out the strips lightly so that they unroll, and leave to dry.

*For lasagne:*
Cut the pasta either into strips about 1 cm/½ inch wide or into rectangles, about 7.5 × 13 cm/3 × 5 inches.

*For cannelloni:*
Cut the pasta into rectangles, approximately 7.5 × 10 cm/3 × 4 inches.

*To cook homemade pasta:*
Drop the pasta into a large quantity of fast boiling salted water. Stir once or twice initially to prevent the pieces sticking together and boil, uncovered, until tender, about 5 minutes. Immediately add cold water to the pan to prevent further cooking, then drain thoroughly and use as required.

Unused pasta can be put into a polythene (plastic) bag and refrigerated overnight, or frozen for up to 1 month.

# TORTELLINI

*Stuffed Pasta Rings*

These delicious stuffed pasta are one of the great special occasion dishes of Emilia-Romagna. Although best served in a good broth, they are sometimes served with *ragù bolognese*, or with butter, cream and grated cheese.

**Metric/Imperial**
40 g/1½ oz butter
175 g/6 oz raw turkey breast meat, sliced
75 g/3 oz cooked ham
75 g/3 oz Mortadella
4 × 15 ml spoons/4 tablespoons grated Parmesan cheese
2 eggs, beaten
salt
freshly ground black pepper
1 recipe homemade egg pasta

Preparing Tortellini from Pasta all' Uova

58

**TO SERVE:**
1.2 litres/2 pints chicken broth
1–2 chicken stock cubes
grated Parmesan cheese

**American**
3 tablespoons butter
6 oz raw turkey breast meat, sliced
3 oz processed ham
3 oz Mortadella
¼ cup grated Parmesan cheese
2 eggs, beaten
salt
freshly ground black pepper
1 recipe homemade egg pasta
**TO SERVE:**
5 cups chicken broth
1–2 chicken bouillon cubes (optional)
grated Parmesan cheese

Melt the butter and fry the turkey slices gently until golden, about 12 minutes. Pass the fried turkey meat, ham and Mortadella through the fine blades of a mincer, twice. Add the cheese and eggs with salt and pepper to taste and mix thoroughly to form a smooth paste. Cover and refrigerate.

Prepare the pasta and roll out very thinly to a large square. Dust lightly with flour and leave to rest and dry for 15 to 20 minutes. Cut into approximately forty 3.5 cm/1½ inch squares and place about 1 × 2.5 cm/1½ spoon/½ teaspoon of filling on each square. Fold each square to form a triangle, enclosing the filling. Press the edges together firmly to seal. Curve each triangle around your fingertip and press the two ends together.

Bring the broth to the boil, adding the stock (bouillon) cubes or seasoning, if necessary. Drop in the tortellini and simmer, stirring occasionally, for 5 minutes. Turn off the heat, cover the pan and leave to stand for 20 to 30 minutes. To serve, ladle the tortellini into soup plates with a little of the broth and pass around grated Parmesan.
SERVES 4

# TAGLIATELLE ALLA BOLOGNESE

*Ribbon Pasta with Bolognese Meat Sauce*

Make the sauce in advance to allow plenty of time for cooking. Incidentally, it is never worth making small quantities of sauce because it freezes well and can be stored in the refrigerator for 2 days.

**Metric/Imperial**
0.5 kg/1 lb bought or homemade tagliatelle (see page 58)
40 g/1½ oz butter
ragù Bolognese (see right)
freshly grated Parmesan cheese

*Tagliatelle alla Bolognese*

**American**
1 lb bought or homemade tagliatelle (see page 58)
3 tablespoons butter
ragù Bolognese (see below)
freshly grated Parmesan cheese
SERVES 4 TO 6

Cook the tagliatelle in plenty of fast boiling salted water until just tender but still *al dente*, about 10 minutes for commercial pasta, 5 minutes for homemade. Drain thoroughly in a colander.

Melt the butter in a hot deep serving dish and add the drained tagliatelle. Add about 4 × 15 ml spoons/4 tablespoons of the hot Bolognese sauce and a little of the cheese, and toss lightly with 2 forks until the pasta is well coated. Pile the remaining sauce on top and serve more grated cheese separately.
SERVES 4 TO 6

# RAGÙ BOLOGNESE

*Bolognese Meat Sauce*

This is the world famous Italian sauce of which there are many variations. It is much richer than the Calabrian meat sauce (page 24), and in Bologna it is generally served with tagliatelle or lasagne, either green or white.

**Metric/Imperial**
15 g/½ oz butter
1 onion, finely chopped
1 small carrot, finely chopped
1 stick celery, finely chopped
3 rashers smoked streaky bacon, derinded and finely chopped
350 g/12 oz finely minced beef
100 g/4 oz chicken livers, finely chopped
4 × 15 ml spoons/4 tablespoons dry white wine or dry vermouth
300 ml/½ pint beef stock
1 × 15 ml spoon/1 tablespoon tomato purée
freshly grated nutmeg
salt
freshly ground black pepper
3 × 15 ml spoons/3 tablespoons double cream or 25 g/1 oz butter (optional)

**American**
1 tablespoon butter
1 onion, finely chopped
1 small carrot, finely chopped
1 stalk celery, finely chopped
3 bacon slices, derinded and finely chopped
1½ cups finely ground beef
¼ lb chicken livers, finely chopped
¼ cup dry white wine or dry vermouth
1¼ cups beef stock
1 tablespoon tomato paste
salt
freshly ground black pepper
3 tablespoons heavy cream or 2 tablespoons butter (optional)

Melt the butter in a large shallow pan. Add the chopped vegetables and bacon and fry gently, stirring frequently, for about 10 minutes until golden. Add the beef and fry, stirring, until it changes colour from red to brown.

Add the chicken livers and cook, stirring for 1 to 2 minutes, then add the wine and simmer until it has almost completely evaporated. Stir in the stock, tomato purée (paste); nutmeg, salt and pepper to taste. Bring to the boil, cover and simmer very gently for 45 minutes to ½ hour, stirring occasionally.

Before serving, stir in the cream or butter, if used, and check the seasoning.
SERVES 6

# LASAGNE AL FORNO

A delicious dish made with well flavoured *ragù* and rich béchamel so that the pasta remains moist and creamy under a bubbling golden crust. It takes time to prepare, but is worth making in double quantities as it freezes and reheats very successfully.

**Metric/Imperial**
1 recipe *ragù Bolognese without cream* (see page 59)
225 g/8 oz green or plain lasagne
salt
BÉCHAMEL SAUCE:
40 g/1½ oz butter
40 g/1½ oz flour
600 ml/1 pint hot milk
4 × 15 ml spoons/4 tablespoons double cream
grated nutmeg
50 g/2 oz Parmesan cheese, freshly grated

**American**
1 recipe *ragù Bolognese, without cream* (see page 59)
½ lb green or plain lasagne
salt
BÉCHAMEL SAUCE:
3 tablespoons butter
⅓ cup flour
2½ cups hot milk
¼ cup heavy cream
grated nutmeg
½ cup freshly grated Parmesan cheese

Prepare the Bolognese sauce in advance. Drop the lasagne into a large pan of fast boiling salted water and boil, stirring from time to time to prevent them sticking together, for about 5 minutes for home-made pasta or according to the packet instructions for commercial pasta. As soon as the lasagne is cooked, add cold water to the pan to stop further cooking. Turn into a colander, then lay the strips side by side on a clean tea towel to drain.

To make the béchamel sauce, melt the butter in a saucepan, stir in the flour and cook for 1 minute. Remove from the heat and pour in the milk and cream, beating continuously with a wire whisk. Return to a high heat and stir until a smooth, thick sauce is formed, then simmer over low heat for 2 to 3 minutes. Season with salt and nutmeg.

Butter a shallow ovenproof serving dish, or a foil dish for freezing, about 20 × 23 cm/8 × 9 inches. Spread a layer of Bolognese sauce over the bottom, cover with an overlapping layer of lasagne, then a layer of béchamel and a sprinkling of grated Parmesan. Repeat the layers, finishing with a thick layer of béchamel and a generous sprinkling of cheese.

Either chill then freeze or, for immediate use, bake in a preheated moderate oven (180°C/350°F, Gas Mark 4) for about 30 minutes until hot through and golden brown on top.
SERVES 7 TO 8

Pinoccate, Petti di Pollo alla Bolognese (below); Lasagne al Forno (above right)

# PETTI DI POLLO ALLA BOLOGNESE

*Chicken Breasts with Ham and Cheese*

A simple, quickly cooked and quite delicious dish that can also be prepared with sliced turkey breast meat or an escalope (scallop) of veal. Cooked (processed) ham can be used instead of prosciutto.

**Metric/Imperial**
4 chicken breasts
salt
freshly ground black pepper
flour for dusting
50 g/2 oz unsalted or clarified butter
1 × 15 ml spoon/1 tablespoon olive oil
4 thin slices of prosciutto
4 × 15 ml spoons/4 tablespoons grated Parmesan cheese
2 × 15 ml spoons/2 tablespoons chopped fresh parsley
4 × 15 ml spoons/4 tablespoons chicken stock
asparagus spears to garnish

**American**
4 chicken breasts
salt
freshly ground black pepper
flour for dusting
¼ cup sweet or clarified butter
1 tablespoon olive oil
4 thin slices of prosciutto
4 tablespoons grated Parmesan cheese
2 tablespoons chopped fresh parsley
¼ cup chicken stock
asparagus spears to garnish

Remove the skin and any bones from the chicken breasts. Lay the chicken breasts flat between two pieces of damp grease-proof (waxed) paper and beat gently with a rolling pin to flatten them. Season with salt and pepper and dust with flour.

Heat the butter and oil in a large heavy frying pan (skillet) and fry the chicken gently, turning once, for about 10 minutes, until golden. On each piece of chicken lay a piece of prosciutto, sprinkle generously with cheese and parsley. Moisten with stock. Cover and cook for 5 minutes.

Arrange the pieces on a serving dish, pour the butter and pan juices over them and garnish with asparagus spears. Serve with a green salad.
SERVES 4

# PINOCCATE

*Almond and Pine Nut Biscuits*

**Metric/Imperial**
75 g/3 oz ground almonds
200 g/7 oz caster sugar
few drops of vanilla essence
pinch of salt
2 medium egg whites
100 g/4 oz pine nuts

**American**
¾ cup ground almonds
⅞ cup sugar
few drops vanilla extract
pinch of salt
2 egg whites
1 cup pine nuts

Pound the almonds and half the sugar to a fine powder with a pestle and mortar or place in an electric blender for about 1 minute on high speed. Turn the mixture into a basin and add the vanilla.

Add the salt to the egg whites and whisk until standing in soft peaks, then beat in the remaining sugar a little at a time. Fold the egg whites lightly but thoroughly into the almond mixture.

Spread the pine nuts on a sheet of greaseproof (waxed) paper. Drop small spoonfuls of the almond mixture onto the nuts, rolling them gently until coated with the nuts. Lightly butter two baking sheets and dust lightly with flour. Arrange the nut-coated pieces about 2.5 cm/1 inch apart on the baking sheets. Bake in a preheated moderately hot oven (200°C/400°F, Gas Mark 6) for about 10 minutes until golden.
MAKES 20 TO 24 BISCUITS

# Liguria

This sunny region consists of a narrow strip of land, often referred to as the Italian Riviera, curving around the top of the Ligurian sea. The port of Genoa sits firmly in the centre, while the region is bounded by the Appenines on the Italian side and the Alps towards France. It is not surprising that such a backcloth and a warm, temperate climate have produced an area of exceptional natural beauty and luxuriant vegetation. Genoese maritime tradition is thought to be partly responsible for the devotion of Ligurians to vegetables and herbs; Columbus reported that sailors returning from long sea voyages had a natural craving for fresh green foods. This was readily satisfied by the abundant locally grown vegetables, and by the aromatic herbs that carpet the hills behind Genoa. Unlike Venice, that other great port also trading in spices from the Far East, the merchants of Genoa seldom used spices in their own cooking, preferring to exchange them for gold. Their cuisine evolved around the use of herbs, vegetables, olive oil and the wide variety of fish and shellfish caught along Liguria's extensive Mediterranean coast.

Flat-leaved parsley, oregano, dill, sage and rosemary all contribute generously to the character of Ligurian cooking, but *the* herb of the area is basil, which the Genoese claim grows better in Liguria than anywhere else in Italy. Bright green, aromatic and spicy basil is the basis of a unique sauce called *pesto*, so named because originally a pestle was used for pounding the herbs and nuts to a paste. The three classic uses of *pesto*, usually listed on menus as *alla Genovese*, are combined with pasta or with *gnocchi* (see page 66), or floating on the surface of the Genoese Minestrone, which contains more vegetables than most versions of this soup. Olive trees flourish in the area in both olive groves and private gardens. Home-grown olives are taken to the local press. The resulting 'green' oil has a wonderfully fresh, fruity flavour, and the quality of 'their' olive oil is a great talking point among neighbours.

The excellent fish dishes are not easy to reproduce in other countries because they are based on Mediterranean species, such as the colourful creatures used in *burrida* (Genoese fish soup) or the *datteri di mare* (sea dates). Squid and cuttlefish are used in a *zimino*, another Genoese fish stew which also contains beet leaves. All these dishes, as well as fish and shellfish that are more familiar to us, ought not to be missed when visiting the area.

Other regional specialities are *cima*, breast of veal rolled around a stuffing of chopped meats, sweetbreads, peas and pistachio nuts; *torta pasqualina*, a flaky pastry tart filled with spinach, artichokes, eggs and cheese; *bigne di pesci misti*, pieces of fish fried in a light batter; *sardenara*, pizza filled with a mixture of onions and tomatoes, topped with olives and anchovies; and last but not least *capon magro*, a great decorative pyramid of boiled and dressed vegetables and fish. A limited amount of pleasant white wine is produced in Liguria, but generally you are more likely to be offered the excellent wines from neighbouring Piemonte.

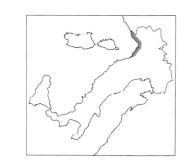

# ZUCCHINI RIPIENI

*Stuffed Courgettes*

These delicately stuffed courgettes (zucchini) make an excellent vegetable course or supper dish. They look most attractive arranged on a shallow circular platter with stuffed mushrooms (see page 20) or stuffed tomatoes (see page 12) in the centre.

**Metric/Imperial**
6 plump courgettes, about 13 cm/5 inches long
salt
25 g/1 oz crustless white bread
milk for soaking
100 g/4 oz Ricotta or soft curd cheese
½ × 2.5 ml spoon/¼ teaspoon dried oregano
1 clove garlic, crushed (optional)
40 g/1½ oz grated Parmesan cheese
1 egg yolk
freshly ground black pepper

**American**
6 plump zucchini, about 5 inches long
salt
1 oz crustless white bread
milk for soaking
¼ lb Ricotta or soft curd cheese
¼ teaspoon dried oregano
1 clove garlic, crushed (optional)
⅓ cup grated Parmesan cheese
1 egg yolk
freshly ground black pepper

Wash and trim the courgettes (zucchini). Drop them into a pan of boiling salted water, simmer for 5 minutes then drain. Meanwhile soak the bread in milk and when soft squeeze it dry. Cut the courgettes (zucchini) in half lengthwise and scoop out the centres, using a teaspoon, leaving long boat-shaped cases for filling.

Chop the centres finely, put into a basin and add the bread, Ricotta, oregano, garlic (if used), Parmesan, egg yolk, several grinds of pepper and about 1 × 2.5 ml spoon/½ teaspoon salt. Mix thoroughly. The consistency should be fairly soft; if too stiff, add a little milk.

Fill the courgette (zucchini) cases and spread the stuffing flat. Arrange close together in a single layer in a well oiled shallow baking tray or dish.

Cook in a preheated moderately hot oven (190°C/375°F, Gas Mark 5) for 35 to 40 minutes until the courgettes (zucchini) are tender and the filling is golden brown.
SERVES 3 TO 4

# FRITTATA CON SPINACI

*Spinach and Egg Omelet*

A *frittata* is made in the same way as an omelet, but instead of being folded it is tossed or turned like a pancake, and served flat. Almost any cooked chopped vegetables or ham or bacon can be added to the eggs to flavour the *frittata*. Spinach is a popular flavouring in Liguria. Make sure the spinach is quite dry before sautéing in butter.

In Italy *frittata* is often served as a garnish for veal escalopes (scallops). The cooked *frittata* is trimmed to the shape of the meat.

**Metric/Imperial**
225 g/8 oz fresh spinach
salt
freshly ground black pepper
pinch of ground nutmeg
25 g/1 oz butter
3 eggs

**American**
½ lb fresh spinach
salt
freshly ground black pepper
pinch of ground nutmeg
2 tablespoons butter
3 eggs

Cook the spinach in a covered saucepan without additional water for 6 to 8 minutes until tender. Drain, and squeeze as dry as possible. Chop coarsely, season with salt, pepper and nutmeg and sauté very gently in half of the butter, stirring frequently, for 5 minutes.

Break the eggs into a basin, season lightly and beat with a fork. Stir in the spinach, mixing well.

Heat the remaining butter in a heavy 18 cm/7 inch frying pan (skillet) and pour in the egg mixture. Cook over high heat for 2 minutes or until lightly set, then toss or turn with a fish slice and cook the underside for a few seconds. Invert on to a plate and serve immediately.
SERVES 1

Frittata con Spinaci, Insalata di Funghi, Zucchini Ripieni

# INSALATA DI FUNGHI

*Raw Mushroom Salad*

Thinly sliced raw mushrooms dressed with olive oil and lemon juice make a delicious starter just as they are or better still topped with a few prawns (shrimp) or chopped anchovy fillets.

Choose firm white button mushrooms and use as soon as possible after purchase for this raw salad.

## Metric/Imperial

225 g/8 oz button mushrooms
1 clove garlic
5 × 15 ml spoons/5 tablespoons olive oil
2 × 15 ml spoons/2 tablespoons lemon juice
freshly ground black pepper
1 × 2.5 ml spoon/½ teaspoon salt
few sprigs of parsley, roughly chopped
175 g/6 oz peeled prawns or 8 anchovy fillets, finely chopped (optional)

## American

2 cups button mushrooms
1 clove garlic
⅓ cup olive oil
2 tablespoons lemon juice
freshly ground black pepper
½ teaspoon salt
few sprigs of parsley, roughly chopped
1 cup shelled shrimp or 8 anchovy filets, finely chopped (optional)

Wipe but do not peel the mushrooms and slice thinly. Cut the garlic clove in half and rub the cut surfaces around a mixing bowl.

Beat the olive oil, lemon juice and pepper together in the bowl. Add the mushrooms and toss gently to mix thoroughly with the dressing. Cover and refrigerate for 1 hour.

Just before serving, add the salt and roughly chopped parsley and toss again. Divide between 4 individual dishes and, if used, scatter the prawns (shrimp) or anchovy pieces over the top.

SERVES 4

# FRITTO MISTO DI MARE

*Mixed Fried Fish*

Pieces of fish encased in *pastella* (light batter) and fried until crisp and golden is a popular dish all around the coast of Italy. The fish used depends entirely on the local catch, but usually includes at least three different species and often more. The shapes and textures should be as varied as possible. A typical Ligurian mixture might include shelled prawns (shrimp), whole but beheaded sardines, rings of squid and small strips of filleted sole. Only the squid needs to be precooked in water before it can be fried.

## Metric/Imperial

BATTER:
100 g/4 oz flour
¼ × 2.5 ml spoon/¼ teaspoon salt
2 × 15 ml spoons/2 tablespoons olive oil
150 ml/¼ pint tepid water
1 large egg white
oil for deep frying
1 kg/2 lb mixed fish, cut into small pieces
TO GARNISH:
lemon and orange wedges
sprigs of parsley

Fritto Misto di Mare (right)

## American

BATTER:
1 cup flour
¼ teaspoon salt
2 tablespoons olive oil
⅔ cup tepid water
1 egg white
oil for deep frying
2 lb mixed fish, cut into small pieces
TO GARNISH:
lemon and orange wedges
sprigs of parsley

To make the batter, sift the flour and salt into a bowl and make a well in the centre. Pour in the oil and gradually beat in the water to form a smooth, thick batter. Refrigerate for about 2 hours. Immediately before using, whisk the egg white stiffly and fold lightly into the batter.

Heat the oil in a deep fryer to 190°C/375°F. Line a baking tin with crumpled kitchen paper towels and heat the oven to moderate for keeping the fish hot.

Fry each type of fish separately, first submerging each piece in batter. Lift out with two skewers, allowing surplus batter to drain off, then lower gently into the oil. Fry for 3 to 6 minutes, depending on the size, turning once.

Lift out with a wire strainer, drain on the crumpled paper and keep hot in the oven until all the fish are fried. Allow the fat to regain frying temperature before frying the next batch.

To serve, pile the fish on a hot serving dish and garnish with lemon and orange wedges and sprigs of parsley.

SERVES 4

# GNOCCHI

*Gnocchi* are eaten in many parts of Italy, but they acquire a local character in Genoa, where they are called *troffie* and served with *pesto* (see below). In other regions, they are served with meat, chicken livers or tomato sauce.

**Metric/Imperial**

0.5 kg/1 lb potatoes, freshly boiled
175 g/6 oz plain flour
1 egg, beaten
salt
freshly ground black pepper
grated nutmeg
TO SERVE:
25 g/1 oz butter
grated Parmesan cheese
pesto sauce (see right)

**American**

1 lb potatoes, freshly boiled
1½ cups all-purpose flour
1 egg, beaten
salt
freshly ground black pepper
grated nutmeg
TO SERVE:
2 tablespoons butter
grated Parmesan cheese
pesto sauce (see right)

Drain the potatoes well to dry thoroughly. Mash very finely (there must be no lumps) and add the flour, egg and salt, pepper and nutmeg to taste. Mix to a dough and turn onto a floured board.

With floured hands, roll pieces of the dough into long sausages, about 1 cm/½ inch in diameter. Cut into 2.5 cm/1 inch lengths and, using your little finger, make a dent in the centre of each one to make them curl slightly.

Drop the *gnocchi*, a few at a time, into a large pan of gently boiling salted water. Cook until they rise to the surface, about 3 to 5 minutes. Lift out with a slotted spoon, drain, put into a buttered dish and keep hot until all are cooked.

Dot with butter and sprinkle with cheese. Thin the *pesto* down with a spoonful or two of the cooking water, then pour it over the *gnocchi* and serve at once.
SERVES 4

# AGLIATA

*Garlic and Bread Sauce*

A powerful seasoning sauce from which it seems likely the much gentler British bread sauce evolved. The Genoese serve *agliata* with fried white fish, beef and liver. A sauce for garlic addicts only!

**Metric/Imperial**

4 cloves garlic
2 × 15 ml spoons/2 tablespoons soft white breadcrumbs
large pinch of salt
1 × 15 ml spoon/1 tablespoon wine vinegar (approximately)

**American**

4 cloves garlic
2 tablespoons soft white bread crumbs
large pinch of salt
1 tablespoon wine vinegar (approximately)

Put the garlic, breadcrumbs and salt into a mortar and pound to a paste. Gradually work in enough vinegar to dilute the paste to the consistency of thick cream.
SERVES 2

# PESTO

*Basil, Nut and Cheese Sauce*

Fresh basil is essential for this famous Genoese speciality. A little parsley can be added to enhance the green colour, if preferred.

**Metric/Imperial**

50 g/2 oz fresh basil leaves
25 g/1 oz pine nuts or walnuts
2 cloves garlic
large pinch of salt
freshly ground black pepper
4 × 15 ml spoons/4 tablespoons olive oil (approximately)
40 g/1½ oz grated Parmesan or Pecorino cheese

**American**

2 oz fresh basil leaves
¼ cup pine nuts or walnuts
2 cloves garlic
large pinch of salt
freshly ground black pepper
¼ cup olive oil (approximately)
½ cup grated Parmesan or Pecorino cheese

Chop the basil and nuts roughly and put into a mortar with the garlic, salt and pepper. Pound together until reduced to a thick paste. Add the oil a little at a time, stirring constantly as for a mayonnaise, until the sauce is the consistency of thick cream.

Alternatively, put the basil, nuts, garlic, salt and pepper into an electric blender with 2 × 15 ml spoons/2 tablespoons of the oil and blend at low speed, adding the remaining oil gradually until a sauce of thick cream consistency is formed.

Stir in the cheese. Keep the sauce covered until required and use fresh.
SERVES 4 TO 6

*To use pesto:*
Before mixing with pasta or *gnocchi*, it is usual to dilute the *pesto* with a little of the water in which the pasta was cooked. In Genoa, *trenette* (a long thin egg pasta) is the favourite for serving with *pesto*, but any ribbon pasta or spaghetti is suitable.

After cooking and draining the pasta, toss with a little butter until each strand glistens. Serve in soup plates with a heaped spoonful of *pesto* on top.

Before eating, mix the sauce with the pasta and sprinkle grated Parmesan or Pecorino liberally on top.

Fricassea di Pollo (right) (page 68)

# FRICASSEA DI POLLO

*Chicken with Egg and Lemon Sauce*

Lemons grow prolifically in Liguria and lemon garnishes are always handy for squeezing over fried fish and grilled (broiled) meats. Lemon juice is the distinctive flavouring of this excellent chicken dish.

**Metric/Imperial**
1 kg/2 lb oven-ready chicken
1 small onion, sliced
1 small carrot, sliced
1 small stick celery, sliced
1 small bay leaf
4 peppercorns
salt
freshly ground black pepper
2 × 15 ml spoons/2 tablespoons oil
25 g/1 oz butter
25 g/1 oz flour
2 egg yolks
juice and thinly pared shredded zest of ½ large lemon
2 × 15 ml spoons/2 tablespoons chopped fresh parsley

**American**
2 lb oven-ready chicken
1 small onion, sliced
1 small carrot, sliced
1 small stalk celery, sliced
1 small bay leaf
4 peppercorns
salt
freshly ground black pepper
2 tablespoons oil
2 tablespoons butter
¼ cup flour
2 egg yolks
juice and thinly pared shredded zest of ½ large lemon
2 tablespoons chopped fresh parsley

Remove the giblets and wash the chicken, then cut into 4 portions.

Put the giblets and backbone into a saucepan with the onion, carrot, celery, bay leaf, peppercorns and 1 × 2.5 ml spoon/½ teaspoon salt. Cover with cold water, bring to the boil, cover and simmer gently for 30 minutes, then strain the stock and reserve 300 ml/½ pint/1¼ cups.

Dry the pieces of chicken and season with salt and pepper. Heat the oil and butter in a wide flameproof pan over low heat and fry the chicken pieces gently, turning occasionally, for about 15 minutes until golden brown. Lift out the chicken and transfer to a plate.

Sprinkle the flour into the pan, stir and cook for 1 minute, then gradually stir in the reserved stock. Bring to the boil, stirring, return the chicken to the pan, cover tightly and simmer for 30 to 40 minutes. Lift out the chicken and arrange on a hot serving dish.

Skim off any surface fat from the chicken sauce. Put the egg yolks and lemon juice into a small basin, add 2 × 15 ml spoons/2 tablespoons of the chicken sauce and beat lightly. Stir into the chicken sauce and heat, without boiling, until lightly thickened. Check the seasoning, pour the sauce over the chicken and serve garnished with strips of lemon zest and parsley.

SERVES 4

# CIMA ALLA GENOVESE

*Stuffed Breast of Veal*

Visitors to Genoa cannot fail to notice this decorative roll of cold stuffed veal on sale in the cooked meat shops and *trattorie*. To make it, seek your butcher's co-operation and ask for a long shaped piece of breast of veal, suitable for making into a bag for stuffing, and weighing 0.75–1 kg/1½–2 lb after boning. Ask him to beat the veal out until it is about 5 mm/¼ inch thick, and to give you the bones separately.

**Metric/Imperial**
0.75–1 kg/1½–2 lb piece of boned breast of veal, prepared as above
salt
freshly ground black pepper
50 g/2 oz crustless bread

# VITELLO ALL' UCCELLETTO

*Sautéed Veal*

Tender milk-fed veal and good olive oil are essential to this speedily prepared dish. There are several versions of the recipe, some cooks insisting that sage is needed to give the meat a 'game' flavour, while others prefer to use bay leaves. Fresh young cooked peas are sometimes added just before serving.

**Metric/Imperial**
0.5 kg/1 lb veal fillet
3 × 15 ml spoons/3 tablespoons olive oil
2 cloves garlic
3–4 bay leaves or 6 fresh sage leaves
salt
freshly ground black pepper
5 × 15 ml spoons/5 tablespoons dry white wine

**American**
1 lb veal filet
3 tablespoons olive oil
2 cloves garlic
3–4 bay leaves or 6 fresh sage leaves
salt
freshly ground black pepper
¼ cup dry white wine

Slice the veal thinly, then beat it out as thinly as possible. Cut into small bite-size pieces, about 2.5 cm/1 inch square.

Heat the oil gently in a large heavy frying pan (skillet) with the garlic and bay or sage leaves, until the oil is well flavoured. Remove from the heat, add the meat and stir until all the pieces are well coated with oil.

Return to a moderately high heat and cook for 3 to 4 minutes, stirring constantly, until the veal is just cooked. Season with salt and pepper, lift out the meat with a slotted spoon and transfer to a hot serving dish. Discard the garlic and herbs.

Add the wine to the frying pan (skillet) and boil briskly, scraping up the juices from the base of the pan, until reduced to a small quantity of syrupy sauce. Spoon over the meat and serve immediately.

SERVES 4

milk for soaking
100 g/4 oz veal sweetbreads
25 g/1 oz butter
50 g/2 oz finely chopped onion
350 g/12 oz shoulder of pork, finely minced
40 g/1½ oz grated Parmesan cheese
½ × 2.5 ml spoon/¼ teaspoon dried marjoram
75 g/3 oz shelled peas
1 artichoke heart, chopped (optional)
25 g/1 oz shelled pistachio nuts (optional)
2 eggs, lightly beaten
2 eggs, hard-boiled
veal bones

### American

1½–2 lb piece of boned breast of veal, prepared as above
salt
freshly ground black pepper
2 oz crustless bread
milk for soaking
¼ lb veal sweetbreads
2 tablespoons butter
⅓ cup finely chopped onion
1½ cups finely ground shoulder of pork
⅓ cup grated Parmesan cheese
¼ teaspoon dried marjoram
½ cup shelled peas
1 artichoke heart, chopped (optional)
¼ cup shelled pistachio nuts (optional)
2 eggs, lightly beaten
2 eggs, hard-cooked
veal bones

Lay the veal flat, season with salt and pepper, fold in half and sew the two longer sides together with thread to form a pocket. Soak the bread in the milk until soft, then squeeze dry. Cover the sweetbreads with cold water, bring to the boil and simmer for 10 minutes, then drain and chop.

Melt the butter in a saucepan and fry the onion gently until beginning to soften. Remove from the heat and add the sweetbreads, bread, pork, cheese, marjoram, peas, artichoke heart, pistachio nuts if used, beaten eggs and a generous seasoning of salt and pepper. Mix together lightly but thoroughly.

Spread half of the stuffing in the veal pocket, arrange the hard-boiled (hard-cooked) eggs on top, and cover with the remaining stuffing. Carefully sew up the opening to enclose the stuffing.

Put the veal bones in a deep saucepan, lay the meat roll on top and cover with cold salted water. Bring to the boil, cover and simmer gently for 1½ to 2 hours. Leave to cool in the water, then drain and refrigerate. Serve cold, cut into fairly thick slices. Use the stock as a basis for soup.

SERVES 10 TO 12

Virello all' Uccelletto, Cima alla Genovese

# Veneto

Veneto lies in the North-Eastern corner of Italy with a long seaboard curving around the head of the Adriatic. The fabled port of Venice dominates the centre of the coastal curve, cradled by the lagoon and its colourful islands. The cooking of Veneto has remained basically Italian in character despite historical links with adjacent countries and trade with the Far East. Although Venice dominates the area and has a culinary tradition of its own, it is easier nowadays to find regional dishes in other cities once ruled by the Venetian Republic. Padua, Vicenza, Verona and Treviso are all gastronomically worth visiting.

Markets are a must for visitors to Veneto. An early morning visit to the fish market alongside Venice's Rialto Bridge reveals a vast array of Mediterranean species. Silvery, whole tuna fish, grey-black eels in boxes, mounds of pale pink Adriatic scampi (jumbo shrimp), scarlet and grey mullet, spiny red crabs, ferocious looking rascasse and angler fish, octopus and squid, and baskets of cream-coloured clams, purple-black mussels and tiny winkles are among the sights that catch the eye. Nearby, the streets are lined with market stalls laden with piles of brilliantly coloured vegetables: red, green, yellow and striped peppers, purple-black aubergine (eggplant), olive-green artichokes, bunches of fresh herbs, courgettes (zucchini), ripe red plum-shaped tomatoes for sauces and round, under-ripe tomatoes for salads. The large yellow flowers of the courgette (zucchini) are sold in bunches to be used for stuffing or made into fritters, a speciality of Padua.

Treviso, to the north of Venice, is the centre of a rich agricultural area and was once the summer retreat for the wealthy aristocracy of Venice, hence the fine architecture and a tradition of good cooking which is still very much alive. A visit to Treviso market involves a leisurely stroll through adjoining squares, each specializing in a particular type of merchandise such as wild mushrooms, poultry and game, fruit and vegetables, until you reach the fish market strategically placed beside a fast flowing canal. A feature of the market in winter is a unique *radiccio rosso*, a type of salad vegetable. Verona market is a daily event in the Piazza delle Erbe, with its stalls beneath striped awnings.

Around the coast, fish and shellfish dishes are the mainstay of the local cuisine. Fish salads are popular, also dried salt cod and dishes made with eels from nearby Comacchio. The people of Veneto have exceptionally hearty appetites and consume vast quantities of polenta, risottos of all kinds and substantial soups. If you are mystified by some of the dishes listed on Venetian menus, these are probably local dialect names and are equally puzzling to Italians from other areas; for example, spaghetti becomes *bigoli*, mussels are *peoci* and ravioli is often *rafoi*.

The Etruscans are said to have planted grapes in the area and today Veneto and the neighbouring regions produce vast quantities of good wine. Several, including Soave, Valpolicella and Bardolino, have become well known outside Italy, but there are many more to discover and enjoy when in the area.

# INSALATA DI RISO CON FRUTTI DI MARE

*Rice and Shellfish Salad*

This well-seasoned rice salad, delicately flavoured with fennel, makes an excellent base for whatever shellfish may be available; cockles or sliced scallops could replace the clams or mussels, for example.

Tuna fish also combines well with the sweet aniseed flavour of fennel and makes a good substitute for shellfish in this dish.

**Metric/Imperial**

RICE SALAD:
225 g/8 oz Italian rice
5 × 15 ml spoons/5 tablespoons olive oil
1 × 15 ml spoon/1 tablespoon lemon juice
1 × 15 ml spoon/1 tablespoon wine vinegar
salt
freshly ground black pepper
1 × 15 ml spoon/1 tablespoon coarsely grated onion
1 large fennel root, trimmed, thinly sliced then shredded
2 × 15 ml spoons/2 tablespoons chopped fresh parsley
SHELLFISH:
1.2 litres/2 pints fresh mussels
1.2 litres/2 pints fresh clams
0.5 kg/1 lb cooked unshelled prawns or scampi
GARNISH:
fennel leaves
2 hard-boiled eggs, quartered lengthwise
black olives (optional)

**American**

RICE SALAD:
1 cup Italian rice
⅓ cup olive oil
1 tablespoon lemon juice
1 tablespoon wine vinegar
salt
freshly ground black pepper
1 tablespoon coarsely grated onion
1 large fennel root, trimmed, thinly sliced, then shredded
2 tablespoons chopped fresh parsley
SHELLFISH:
5 cups fresh mussels
5 cups fresh clams
1 lb cooked unshelled shrimp or jumbo shrimp
GARNISH:
fennel leaves
2 hard-cooked eggs, quartered lengthwise
ripe olives (optional)

Add the rice to a large saucepan containing plenty of fast boiling salted water and cook until just tender. Drain thoroughly, put into a basin and add the oil, lemon juice, vinegar, salt, pepper and onion. Toss lightly until well mixed and set aside until cold. Fold the fennel into the rice with the parsley. Check the seasoning.

Scrape and scrub the mussels in cold water. Remove the beard and discard any mussels that are cracked or do not shut tightly when given a sharp tap. Rinse in cold water and drain. Put into a wide saucepan, cover and place over a moderately high heat, shaking the pan frequently until the mussels begin to open, about 5 minutes. As they open, transfer them to a colander.

When cool remove most of the mussels from their shells, leaving a few unshelled for garnishing.

Prepare and cook the clams in the same way. Shell most of the clams and prawns (shrimp) or scampi (jumbo shrimp), reserving a few of each for decoration.

Fold the cold shellfish into the rice and pile into the centre of a serving dish. Top with a few unshelled prawns (shrimp) and sprays of fennel leaves. Garnish with the hard-boiled (hard-cooked) eggs, olives if used, and the reserved shellfish.
SERVES 4

# RISOTTO VERONESE

*Verona Style Risotto*

Throughout the Veneto region, risotto is a basic dish flavoured with whatever happens to be available, for example: pieces of cooked chicken, game, fish, cooked ham or chicken livers.

For *risotto bianco*, prepare as for *Risotto alla Milanese* (page 82) but omit the saffron.

**Metric/Imperial**

risotto bianco (see above)
4 chicken livers
25 g/1 oz butter
50 g/2 oz cooked ham, finely diced
25 g/1 oz grated Parmesan cheese
TO SERVE:
Verona-style mushrooms (see page 73)

**American**

risotto bianco (see above)
4 chicken livers
2 tablespoons butter
¼ cup finely diced processed ham
¼ cup Parmesan cheese
TO SERVE:
Verona-style mushrooms (see page 73)

Prepare the risotto. Wash the chicken livers, discarding any tissues or discoloured areas, and cut into small pieces.

Melt the butter, fry the chopped livers very gently for 2 to 3 minutes until lightly cooked, then add the ham. Stir into the risotto with the Parmesan cheese. Serve with Verona-style mushrooms.
SERVES 4

Insalata di Riso con Frutti di Mare

# ZUPPA DI PESCE

*Fish Soup*

The excellent fish soups found all along the Adriatic are more like stews than soups in consistency and are served with a fork as well as a spoon. As some of the fish normally included are unlikely to be available in other countries, use a good mixture of any firm fish such as red and grey mullet, sea bass, mackerel, sole or rock fish.

**Metric/Imperial**

1.5 kg/3 lb assorted fish (see above)
600 ml/1 pint cold water
salt
4 × 15 ml spoons/4 tablespoons olive oil
2 large onions, thinly sliced
2 sticks celery, thinly sliced
2 large cloves garlic, finely chopped
2 × 15 ml spoons/2 tablespoons chopped fresh parsley
1 × 5 ml spoon/1 teaspoon tomato purée
freshly ground black pepper
150 ml/¼ pint dry white wine
350 g/12 oz tomatoes, seeded and roughly chopped
100 g/4 oz cooked peeled small scampi or prawns
6 slices French bread, fried in oil until crisp and golden

**American**

3 lb assorted fish (see above)
2½ cups cold water
salt
¼ cup olive oil
2 large onions, thinly sliced
2 stalks celery, thinly sliced
2 large cloves garlic, finely chopped
2 tablespoons chopped fresh parsley
¾ cup dry white wine
1 teaspoon tomato paste
freshly ground black pepper
1½ cups seeded and roughly chopped tomatoes
⅔ cup cooked shelled small jumbo shrimp or shrimp
6 slices French bread, fried in oil until crisp and golden

Clean and fillet the fish, removing the heads and tails. Put the fish heads, tails and trimmings into a saucepan, add the water and a little salt, bring to the boil and simmer gently for 30 minutes. Strain and reserve the stock.

Heat the oil in a large flameproof casserole and fry the onions, celery and garlic gently until soft and golden. Add the parsley and wine and allow to bubble for several minutes until the liquor has reduced by about half. Add the tomatoes, tomato purée (paste), fish stock and salt and pepper to taste, and simmer for 15 minutes.

Cut the fish into thick slices, add to the casserole and simmer gently for 10 minutes. Add the scampi (jumbo shrimp) or prawns (shrimp) and simmer for another 3 to 5 minutes or until all the fish are cooked.

Check the seasoning and spoon the fish soup into hot soup bowls, each containing a slice of fried bread.

SERVES 6

Zuppa di Pesce

1 × 15 ml spoon/1 tablespoon flour
squeeze of lemon juice
salt
freshly ground black pepper

**American**

2 cups button mushrooms
1 tablespoon olive oil
3 tablespoons butter
¼ cup finely chopped onion
1 clove garlic, crushed
2 tablespoons chopped fresh parsley
1 tablespoon flour
squeeze of lemon juice
salt
freshly ground black pepper

Wash and drain, but do not peel, the mushrooms, then slice them very finely. Heat the oil and 25 g/1 oz/2 tablespoons of the butter in a small saucepan and fry the onion, garlic and parsley gently for about 6 minutes.

Sprinkle in the flour and cook for 1 minute, then stir in the mushrooms and simmer gently for about 1 to 2 minutes until they are tender. Add the lemon juice, salt and pepper to taste, and stir in the remaining butter.

SERVES 4

# FUNGHI IN UMIDO ALLA VERONESE

*Verona Style Mushrooms*

Sliced mushrooms cooked in this manner are excellent served with buttered pasta, grilled chicken or Risotto Veronese.

**Metric/Imperial**

225 g/8 oz button mushrooms
1 × 15 ml spoon/1 tablespoon olive oil
40 g/1½ oz butter
50 g/2 oz finely chopped onion
1 clove garlic, crushed
2 × 15 ml spoons/2 tablespoons chopped fresh parsley

# TIMBALLO DI RISO CON SCAMPI E FUNGHI

*Rice with Scampi (jumbo shrimp) and Mushrooms*

**Metric/Imperial**
225 g/8 oz Italian rice
salt
100 g/4 oz butter
1 bay leaf
0.5 kg/1 lb shelled scampi
2 × 15 ml spoons/2 tablespoons brandy
3 × 15 ml spoons/3 tablespoons flour
150 ml/¼ pint milk
1 × 15 ml spoon/1 tablespoon tomato
  purée
300 ml/½ pint single cream
freshly ground black pepper
1 × 15 ml spoon/1 tablespoon oil
225 g/8 oz button mushrooms
squeeze of lemon juice
3 × 15 ml spoons/3 tablespoons grated
  Parmesan cheese
GARNISH:
chopped fresh parsley
lemon wedges

**American**
1 cup Italian rice
salt
½ cup butter
1 bay leaf
2⅔ cup shelled jumbo shrimp
2 tablespoons brandy
3 tablespoons flour
⅔ cup milk
1 tablespoon tomato paste
1¼ cups light cream
freshly ground black pepper
1 tablespoon oil
2 cups button mushrooms
squeeze of lemon juice
3 tablespoons grated Parmesan cheese
GARNISH:
chopped fresh parsley
lemon wedges

Add the rice to a saucepan containing plenty of boiling salted water and cook until just tender, then drain. Meanwhile heat 40 g/1½ oz/3 tablespoons butter in a saucepan, add the bay leaf and scampi (jumbo shrimp) and cook, stirring, over gentle heat for 1 to 2 minutes. Add the brandy and simmer until it has evaporated, then stir in the flour and cook for 1 minute.

In another pan, heat the oil with 25 g/1 oz/2 tablespoons butter and sauté the

mushrooms gently for 5 minutes, tossing frequently, then season with salt and sprinkle with lemon juice.

Add the cheese and remaining butter to the rice and toss with a fork until well mixed. Pack the rice firmly into a well oiled ring mould, then turn out onto a hot serving dish. Fill the centre with the scampi (jumbo shrimp) sauce and arrange the mushrooms around the rice. Sprinkle these with parsley and tuck the lemon wedges in between the mushrooms. Serve immediately.
SERVES 4

# SOGLIOLE ALLA VENEZIANA

*Venetian Style Sole*

A modern version of an ancient Venetian sweet-sour recipe for sole, and an interesting way to serve lesser flat fish such as dab.

**Metric/Imperial**
4 small flat fish, each about 350 g/12 oz
seasoned flour for coating
olive oil for shallow frying
1 onion, finely chopped
1 stick celery, finely chopped
3 × 15 ml spoons/3 tablespoons
  sultanas
2 × 15 ml spoons/2 tablespoons pine
  nuts
150 ml/¼ pint white wine vinegar
150 ml/¼ pint water
salt
freshly ground black pepper
1 × 15 ml spoon/1 tablespoon chopped
  fresh parsley (optional)

**American**
4 small flat fish, each about ¾ lb
seasoned flour for coating
olive oil for shallow frying
1 onion, finely chopped
1 stalk celery, finely chopped
3 tablespoons seedless white raisins
2 tablespoons pine nuts
⅔ cup white wine vinegar
⅔ cup water
salt

freshly ground black pepper
1 tablespoon chopped fresh parsley
  (optional)

Ask the fishmonger to remove the heads, trim and skin the fish. Rinse them in cold water, pat dry and coat with seasoned flour. Heat the oil in a heavy frying pan (skillet) and fry the fish gently for 3 to 4 minutes on each side, until cooked through and golden. Drain and keep hot.

Heat 3 × 15 ml spoons/3 tablespoons oil in a small pan and fry the onion and celery gently until soft, then add the sultanas (seedless white raisins) nuts, vinegar, water and salt and pepper to taste. Bring to the boil and simmer, uncovered, for 10 minutes until the fruit is plump and the liquor is well reduced. Spoon over the fish, sprinkle with parsley if liked, and serve immediately.
SERVES 4

# ANGUILLA CON PEPERONI ALLA VENETA

*Eel with Peppers and Tomatoes*

The peppers and tomatoes counteract the richness of the eel and give a colourful dish. Choose a medium-sized eel if possible.

**Metric/Imperial**
225 g/8 oz yellow peppers
4 × 15 ml spoons/4 tablespoons olive oil
2 large cloves garlic, sliced
1 kg/2 lb eel, cleaned, skinned and cut
  into 7.5 cm/3 inch pieces
salt
freshly ground black pepper
6 × 15 ml spoons/6 tablespoons dry
  white wine
0.5 kg/1 lb tomatoes, skinned, seeded
  and chopped
1 × 5 ml spoon/1 teaspoon chopped
  fresh parsley

**American**

¼ lb yellow peppers

¼ cup olive oil

2 large cloves garlic, sliced

2 lb eel, cleaned, skinned and cut into
   3 inch pieces

salt

freshly ground black pepper

6 tablespoons dry white wine

2 cups skinned, seeded and chopped
   tomatoes

1 teaspoon chopped fresh parsley

Grill (broil) the sweet peppers under
a moderate heat, turning occasionally,
until the skins are charred. When cool,
peel and cut into fine strips, discarding the
stem and seeds.

Heat the oil in a wide saucepan and fry
the garlic gently for 1 minute. Add the
pieces of eel and fry until lightly browned,
then season with salt and pepper. Add the
wine and allow to bubble until almost
completely reduced. Press the tomato pulp
through a sieve (strainer) into the pan and
simmer for 15 to 20 minutes. Stir in the
strips of pepper and heat through.

Arrange the eel on an oval serving dish,
spoon over the sauce and sprinkle with
parsley.

SERVES 6

## FEGATO ALLA VENEZIANA

*Venetian Style Liver*

Although basically a dish of fried liver
and onions, prepared in the Venetian
way the dish has a flavour and character
all its own. If calves' (veal) liver is not
available, try young pigs' liver, thinly
sliced, then blanched in boiling water,
drained and dried. Allow a little extra
cooking time for pigs' liver.

**Metric/Imperial**

5 × 15 ml spoons/5 tablespoons olive oil

275 g/10 oz onions, very thinly sliced

0.5 kg/1 lb liver

salt

freshly ground black pepper

GARNISH:

1 × 15 ml spoon/1 tablespoon chopped
   fresh parsley

4 lemon wedges (optional)

**American**

⅓ cup olive oil

2½ cups very thinly sliced onions

1 lb liver

salt

freshly ground black pepper

GARNISH:

1 tablespoon chopped fresh parsley

4 lemon wedges (optional)

Heat the oil in a large heavy frying pan
(skillet) and fry the onions gently, covered
but stirring frequently, for about 20
minutes until soft and golden.

Slice the liver horizontally into wafer
thin slices, then cut each slice into small
pieces roughly 5 cm/2 inches square.
Season the onions with salt and pepper,
increase the heat, add the liver and fry
quickly, uncovered, stirring often, for
about 2 minutes, until the liver is just
cooked but still pink inside.

Serve immediately, garnished with
parsley and lemon wedges if used.

SERVES 4

Fegato alla Veneziana, Timballo di Riso
con Scampi e Funghi, Sogliole alla
Veneziana

# MAIALE AL LATTE
## Pork Cooked in Milk

There are many variations on this original and excellent way of cooking pork. The flavouring can be a sprig of rosemary, or a few chopped leaves of marjoram, basil or fennel. About 100 g/4 oz mushrooms, sliced and sautéed in butter, can be added to the sauce at the end of the cooking.

**Metric/Imperial**
1 kg/2 lb boneless leg or loin of pork, derinded
salt
freshly ground black pepper
1 clove garlic, crushed
4 coriander seeds, crushed
40 g/1½ oz butter
1.2 litres/2 pints milk

**American**
2 lb boneless leg or loin of pork, derinded
salt
freshly ground black pepper
1 clove garlic, crushed
4 coriander seeds, crushed
3 tablespoons butter
5 cups milk

Ask the butcher for a piece of lean pork that can be rolled and tied into a sausage shape. Season the inside of the meat with salt and pepper and sprinkle with the garlic and coriander. Roll up and tie securely with string. Melt the butter in a deep, heavy based saucepan or flameproof casserole into which the meat fits fairly closely. Brown the meat over gentle heat, turning to brown all surfaces.

In another pan, bring the milk just to the boil. When the meat has browned, pour the milk over it; there should be just enough milk to cover. Simmer gently, uncovered, for about 1 hour.

Stir the skin that will have formed into the rest of the milk and continue cooking for 30 to 45 minutes, until the meat is tender and the milk reduced to about 250 ml/⅓ pint/1 cup. Lift out the meat, slice and arrange in a hot, shallow serving dish and keep hot.

Beat the milk remaining in the pan lightly and scrape the juices from the bottom of the pan. It should be beige in colour, grainy in texture and creamy in consistency; if not, cook for a few more minutes, taking care that it does not catch and burn. Spoon over the slices of pork and serve hot or cold.
SERVES 6

# POLENTA CON OSELETI SCAMPAI
## Polenta with Skewered Meats

This is a very substantial, traditional Venetian dish. For most appetites the veal can be omitted.

Fresh sage leaves give the meat a characteristic flavour. If unobtainable, sprinkle a little dried sage over the meat before cooking.

**Metric/Imperial**
cold thick polenta (see page 82)
225 g/8 oz veal sweetbreads, soaked in cold water for 1 to 2 hours
4 thick slices pickled belly pork
75 g/3 oz butter
6 chicken livers, halved
225 g/8 oz slice of veal fillet
16 small flat mushrooms
8 fresh sage leaves
salt
freshly ground black pepper
GARNISH:
4 lemon wedges

**American**
cold thick polenta (see page 82)
½ lb veal sweetbreads, soaked in cold water for 1 to 2 hours
4 thick slices pickled salt pork
6 tablespoons butter
6 chicken livers, halved
½ lb slice of veal filet
16 small flat mushrooms
8 fresh sage leaves
salt
freshly ground black pepper
GARNISH:
4 lemon wedges

Polenta con Oseleti Scampai; Maiale al Latte

Spread the polenta in a circle, approximately 2 cm/¾ inch thick. Cut into 4 triangular pieces. Drain the sweetbreads, cover with fresh cold water, bring slowly to the boil and simmer for 15 minutes. Drain, immerse in cold water and peel away all skin and fat, then cut into 12 equal pieces.

Cut each slice of pork into 4 pieces. Place in a saucepan, cover with cold water and bring to the boil. Simmer for 15 minutes, then drain. Melt 25 g/1 oz/2 tablespoons butter in a saucepan and fry the chicken livers for about 2 minutes, turning to seal all sides, then drain. Beat out the veal until no more than 5 mm/¼ inch thick, then cut into 3 cm/1¼ inch squares.

Divide the meats into 4 equal portions. Thread the pieces of meat and mushrooms alternately onto 4 kebab skewers, starting

and ending with pork and inserting a sage leaf occasionally. Season lightly with salt and generously with pepper. Melt 25 g/1 oz/2 tablespoons butter in the pan in which the livers were fried and use to brush the kebabs. Grill (broil) the kebabs under a preheated grill (broiler) for about 10 minutes, turning several times and brushing with melted butter frequently to ensure the meat does not become dry.

Fry the polenta slices gently in the remaining butter until hot through and golden brown on each side. To serve, arrange the polenta slices in a hot serving dish, and lay the kebabs on top. Garnish with lemon wedges. Remove the meats from the skewers at the table and squeeze the lemon over them.
SERVES 4

Aranci Caramellizzati (below right)

# ARANCI CARAMELLIZZATI

*Caramelized Oranges*

A Venetian chef is reputed to have invented this refreshing and colourful dessert using large Sicilian seedless oranges.

**Metric/Imperial**
6 large seedless oranges
225 g/8 oz granulated sugar
300 ml/½ pint water
1 × 15 ml spoon/1 tablespoon Arum or another orange liqueur (optional)

**American**
6 large seedless oranges
1 cup sugar
1⅓ cups water
1 tablespoon Arum or other orange liqueur (optional)

Thinly pare the rind from one orange, with a potato peeler. Shred the rind finely and simmer in just enough water to cover, for 8 minutes or until tender. Drain. Using a serrated knife, peel the rind, pith and skin from the oranges, leaving the flesh exposed.

Place the sugar and 150 ml/¼ pint/⅔ cup of the water in a pan over low heat. Stir until completely dissolved, then boil for a few minutes until cloudy. Remove from the heat, add the oranges, 3 at a time, and spoon the syrup over them. Lift out and arrange in a serving dish.

Add the strips of rind to the remaining syrup and heat gently until the syrup begins to caramelize and turn pale gold. Quickly take the pan off the heat and stand in a bowl of warm water to stop further cooking. Put a little of the caramelized rind on top of each orange.

Add the remaining 150 ml/¼ pint/⅔ cup water, and the orange liqueur if used, to the pan and heat, stirring, until the caramel dissolves. Leave until cold then pour over the oranges. Serve slightly chilled.
SERVES 6

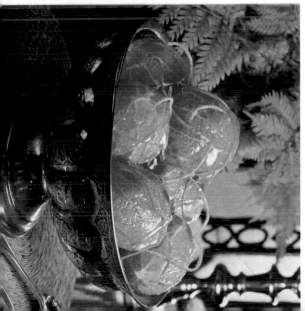

# Lombardy

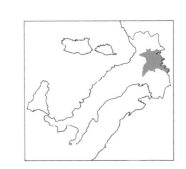

Lombardy is a large region stretching from the Alps in the North to the valley of the river Po in the South. It includes most of the Italian lakes and their breath-taking scenery, as well as acres and acres of fertile pasture land. It is here in the lowlands that huge herds of dairy cows graze contentedly and yield vast quantities of rich milk. The milk provides the basis for the manufacture of the two famous cheeses of Lombardy, Gorgonzola and Bel Paese, as well as other less well known ones such as Stracchino and Taleggio.

Before the invention of modern cookers and convenience foods, the characteristic of Milanese cooking was that of dishes cooked long and slowly over a gentle fire. Today, standing in awe of the fast-moving traffic in the centre of industrial Milan, it is hard to credit such a tradition, but here and there it still survives and resists the onslaught of new methods. The butter provided by the dairy herds is another good reason for slow cooking, and butter, not oil, is the preferred cooking medium in Lombardy. The braised meat dishes, risottos, polenta, soups and peperonata are all evidence of an 'over the fire' cooking tradition.

Vegetables are cultivated in large quantities and much used in home cooking. Huge pots of minestrone, thick with vegetables and herbs, are found simmering in kitchens. These are prepared in large quantities so that they will be sufficient for tonight's meal and, with extra rice or pasta added, for tomorrow as well. In the warm weather the soup is eaten *semi-freddo*, or lukewarm. Substance is added to meals with risotto or polenta rather than with potatoes or pasta.

Based on the round-grain rice grown in the Po valley, risotto is one of the great dishes of the Lombardy kitchen and is always served as a dish on its own. The one traditional exception is the saffron-coloured *Risotto Milanese* served with *Ossobuco*. A basic risotto can have many ingredients added to it and is a classic example of the Italian housewife's genius for making small amounts of poultry, meat or fish into attractive dishes. Leftover risotto is fried crisp in the form of a thick pancake known as *risotto al salto*.

The favourite meat of Lombardy is veal and many of the finest Italian veal dishes originated here. These include recipes for the cheaper cuts such as shin or breast of veal as well as for the more expensive fillet and cutlets. Turkeys are reared in Lombardy and a recipe for turkey with a chestnut and fruit stuffing is given in this chapter. Travellers passing through Lombardy are likely to be offered a slice of *panettone*, a tall, lightly fruited yeast cake, with their coffee; at Easter, a bun called *colomba* is made from the same mixture.

Although not a great wine region, some delightful wines are produced in the Valtellina valley, including such noteworthy light red wines as Sasella, Inferno and Grumello. Pleasant white wines are made on the western shores of Lake Garda and are mostly drunk in the area. Devotees of Campari are quick to point out that this aperitif was first concocted in Milan by a member of the Campari family.

# MINESTRONE ALLA CASALINGA

*Homestyle Minestrone*

Every Italian housewife composes her own minestrone according to the vegetables in season. It is invariably thick with vegetables, scented with herbs and seasoned by stirring in a little grated Parmesan or Pecorino cheese just before serving. In the Milanese version, rice is substituted for the pasta.

Minestrone alla Casalinga

**Metric/Imperial**
100 g/4 oz haricot beans
3 × 15 ml spoons/3 tablespoons oil
2 onions, chopped
2 cloves garlic, crushed
2–3 rashers bacon
4 tomatoes, skinned, seeded and chopped
1.75 litres/3 pints water
1 × 5 ml spoon/1 teaspoon chopped fresh marjoram
1 × 2.5 ml spoon/½ teaspoon chopped fresh thyme
2 carrots, diced
2 potatoes, diced
1 small turnip, diced
1–2 sticks celery, finely sliced
225 g/8 oz cabbage, shredded
50 g/2 oz macaroni pieces or small pasta – shells, stars, etc.
1 × 15 ml spoon/1 tablespoon chopped fresh parsley
salt
freshly ground black pepper
grated Parmesan cheese

**American**
½ cup navy beans
3 tablespoons oil
2 onions, chopped
2 cloves garlic, crushed
2–3 bacon slices
4 tomatoes, skinned, seeded and chopped
7½ cups water
1 teaspoon chopped fresh marjoram
½ teaspoon chopped fresh thyme
2 carrots, diced
2 potatoes, diced
1 small turnip, diced
1–2 stalks celery, finely sliced
3 cups shredded cabbage
½ cup macaroni pieces or small pasta – shells, stars, etc.
1 tablespoon chopped fresh parsley
salt
freshly ground black pepper
grated Parmesan cheese

Soak the beans overnight.
Heat the oil in a large saucepan, add the onions, garlic and bacon and sauté for a few minutes. Add the tomatoes and haricot (navy) beans. Add the water, marjoram and thyme and simmer for about 2 hours, covered.

Add the carrots, cook for about 10 minutes, then add the potatoes and turnip. Cook for a few more minutes, then add the celery, cabbage and pasta. Cook until the pasta and all the vegetables are tender, then add the parsley and salt and pepper to taste.

Stir in 2 or 3 × 15 ml spoons/2 or 3 tablespoons grated Parmesan, and offer extra cheese when serving.
SERVES 4 TO 6

# PEPERONATA

*Peppers with Tomatoes and Onions*

This colourful dish of vegetables, served cold, makes a homely antipasto. Served hot as a vegetable, it goes well with roast or grilled chicken, lamb or pork. The flavour of the sweet peppers should predominate, but otherwise Italians vary the recipe according to what is available. For instance, celery is often added, but if tomatoes become expensive they are simply left out.

**Metric/Imperial**
6 large peppers, red, yellow, green or mixed
4 × 15 ml spoons/4 tablespoons oil
225 g/8 oz onions, chopped
2 cloves garlic, sliced
2 bay leaves
0.5 kg/1 lb tomatoes, skinned and quartered
salt
freshly ground black pepper

**American**
6 large peppers, red, yellow, green or mixed
¼ cup oil
2 cups chopped onions
2 cloves garlic, sliced
2 bay leaves
1 lb tomatoes, skinned and quartered
salt
freshly ground black pepper

SERVES 4

Cut the peppers lengthwise in half, discard the stem, pith and seeds and rinse in cold water. Cut the flesh into 1 cm/½ inch wide strips. Heat the oil in a wide pan and fry the onions, garlic and bay leaves gently for about 5 minutes, stirring now and then. Add the peppers to the pan, stir, cover and cook gently for about 10 minutes. Add the tomatoes with a little salt and pepper and cook uncovered, stirring frequently, until most of the liquid has evaporated and the peperonata is fairly thick; this may take up to 30 minutes, depending on the tomatoes. Remove the bay leaves, check the seasoning and serve cold or hot.

## PESCE IN CARPIONE

*Fried Marinated Fish*

The lakes of Lombardy abound with fish. Marinating fish after frying is a good way of adding flavour to freshwater varieties or to eel or rock salmon.

**Metric/Imperial**
0.5 kg/1 lb filleted fish
little milk
seasoned flour for coating
oil for shallow frying
MARINADE:
2 × 15 ml spoons/2 tablespoons oil
1 small onion, thinly sliced
1 large clove garlic, crushed
1 yellow or green pepper, grilled, skinned and seeded
4 × 15 ml spoons/4 tablespoons dry white wine
2 × 15 ml spoons/2 tablespoons wine vinegar
3 fresh sage leaves
1 × 5 ml spoon/1 teaspoon sugar
salt
freshly ground black pepper

**American**
1 lb fileted fish
little milk
seasoned flour for coating
oil for shallow frying
MARINADE:
2 tablespoons oil
1 small onion, thinly sliced
1 large clove garlic, crushed
1 yellow or green pepper, broiled, skinned and seeded
¼ cup dry white wine
2 tablespoons wine vinegar
3 fresh sage leaves
1 teaspoon sugar
salt
freshly ground black pepper

Discard any skin or bones from the fish and cut the flesh into 2.5 cm/1 inch wide strips. Dip in milk, drain and then coat in seasoned flour.

Heat enough oil in a shallow frying pan (skillet) to give a depth of about 5 mm/¼ inch, and fry the fish until crisp and golden on both sides and cooked through. Drain on crumpled kitchen paper towels and arrange closely, side by side, in a shallow serving dish.

To prepare the marinade, heat the oil in a saucepan and fry the onion and garlic very gently for about 8 minutes until soft and golden. Cut the pepper into fine strips, add to the onion and fry for 3 to 4 minutes, then add the wine, vinegar, sage leaves, sugar, and salt and pepper to taste. Bring to the boil, simmer for 1 to 2 minutes then pour over the fish.

Cover and leave in a cold place overnight. Serve cold as an antipasto.
SERVES 3 TO 4

Peperonata, Pesce in Carpione

*Lombardy*

# RISOTTO ALLA MILANESE

*Milanese Risotto*

Unlike most rice dishes, an Italian risotto has a moist, creamy texture. This is the result of using the very absorbent, plump, round-grain rice grown in the Po valley; varieties such as Arborio or Vialone are usually stocked by Italian delicatessen stores. The beef marrow and saffron are traditional, but not essential, ingredients.

**Metric/Imperial**

50 g/2 oz butter
100 g/4 oz onion, finely chopped
25 g/1 oz beef marrow (optional)
350 g/12 oz Italian rice
4 × 15 ml spoons/4 tablespoons white wine
1.2 litres/2 pints hot chicken stock
½ × 2.5 ml spoon/¼ teaspoon powdered saffron (optional)
2 × 15 ml spoons/2 tablespoons grated Parmesan cheese
salt
freshly ground black pepper
TO SERVE:
grated Parmesan cheese

**American**

¼ cup butter
1 cup finely chopped onion
1 oz beef marrow (optional)
2 cups Italian rice
¼ cup white wine
5 cups hot chicken stock
¼ teaspoon powdered saffron (optional)
2 tablespoons grated Parmesan cheese
salt
freshly ground black pepper
TO SERVE:
grated Parmesan cheese

Melt 25 g/1 oz of the butter in a heavy based saucepan and fry the onion gently for about 7 minutes until soft and golden. Add the marrow, if used, and the rice and stir until the rice is translucent. Add the wine and cook until almost completely absorbed. Then begin stirring in the hot stock, a little at a time, adding more as soon as the previous addition is almost absorbed. Stir frequently, and cook uncovered over moderate heat.

Towards the end of the cooking add the saffron, if used, dissolved in 1 × 15 ml spoon/1 tablespoon of the hot stock. Stir in the remaining butter, the Parmesan cheese and salt and pepper to taste.

The risotto is ready to serve when the rice is tender but firm and the consistency of the dish is creamy. Untreated Italian rice takes from 20 to 25 minutes to cook. Serve with extra Parmesan cheese.

SERVES 4

# POLENTA

Polenta, a type of thick porridge made with maize flour, is still a staple food of Northern Italy as in Roman times. It is usually made in sufficient quantity to ensure that enough is left over to fry for the next meal. Maize flour is available in most Italian stores.

**Metric/Imperial**

750 ml/1¼ pints water
2 × 5 ml spoons/2 teaspoons salt
225 g/8 oz finely ground polenta
freshly ground black pepper

**American**

3 cups water
2 teaspoons salt
½ lb finely ground polenta
freshly ground black pepper

Bring the water and salt to a steady boil in a saucepan. Slowly pour in the polenta, stirring all the time with a wooden spoon until a smooth mixture forms. Lower the heat and simmer, stirring frequently, for 20 to 25 minutes or until it resembles thick porridge. Add pepper to taste.

If a thicker polenta is required, continue cooking over very low heat until almost too thick to stir.

Serve 'porridge' consistency polenta with a meat, tomato or mushroom sauce poured over, and hand grated Parmesan separately.

Thick or leftover polenta is shaped on a wooden board into a flat cake about 2.5 cm/1 inch thick. When cold, it is cut into slices and fried, grilled (broiled) or baked and served with small roast birds or with a hot sauce.

SERVES 4

# ANITRA ARROSTO AL MARSALA

*Roast Duck with Marsala*

Although not listed as a traditional Lombardy dish, I first sampled this excellent way of cooking duck in Milan and therefore added it to this region.

**Metric/Imperial**

1.75–2.25 kg/4–5 lb oven-ready duck
salt
freshly ground black pepper
1 small onion
7 fresh sage leaves, crushed, or 3 × 2.5 ml spoons/1½ teaspoons dried sage
3 × 15 ml spoons/3 tablespoons Marsala
150 ml/¼ pint stock or water
juice of ¼ lemon

**American**

4–5 lb oven-ready duck
salt
freshly ground black pepper
1 small onion
7 fresh sage leaves, crushed, or 1½ teaspoons dried sage
3 tablespoons Marsala
⅔ cup stock or water
juice of ¼ lemon

Remove the giblets and wash and dry the duck. Sprinkle the inside of the duck with salt and pepper and insert the onion and half of the sage. Prick the skin of the duck to release the fat while cooking, then rub with the remaining sage.

Place the duck breast down in a roasting tin with the giblets around it. Cook in the centre of a preheated moderate oven (160°C/325°F, Gas Mark 3) for 30 minutes.

Turn breast upwards and pour over the Marsala. Continue roasting, basting with the pan juices now and then, for 1 hour.

Raise the oven temperature to moderately hot (200°C/400°F, Gas Mark 6) and continue cooking for another 30 minutes or until the skin is crisp and golden brown. Transfer the duck to a serving dish and keep hot.

Skim off surplus fat from the roasting tin, add the stock or water and the lemon juice, bring to a fast boil on top of the cooker and check the seasoning. Strain the sauce into a hot dish and serve with the duck.

Serve on a bed of watercress, with braised celery or fennel, if liked.
SERVES 4

*Risotto alla Milanese, Anitra Arrosto al Marsala, Polenta*

# INVOLTINI DI PETTI DI POLLO

*Stuffed Chicken Breasts*

An excellent dish to make during the asparagus season, or throughout the year using canned or frozen asparagus.

**Metric/Imperial**
4 chicken breasts
salt
freshly ground black pepper
4 thin small slices cooked ham
4 thin slices Bel Paese cheese
4 cooked asparagus spears
flour for dusting
40 g/1½ oz butter
1 × 15 ml spoon/1 tablespoon oil
6 × 15 ml spoons/6 tablespoons Marsala
2 × 15 ml spoons/2 tablespoons chicken stock
cooked or canned asparagus spears to garnish

**American**
4 chicken breasts
salt
freshly ground black pepper
4 thin small slices processed ham
4 thin slices Bel Paese cheese
4 cooked asparagus spears
flour for dusting
3 tablespoons butter
1 tablespoon oil
6 tablespoons Marsala
2 tablespoons chicken stock
cooked or canned asparagus spears to garnish

Remove any skin and bones from the chicken breasts. Lay them flat between pieces of damp greaseproof (waxed) paper and beat with a rolling pin until thin. Season with salt and pepper and place a slice of ham on each, then a slice of cheese and an asparagus spear. Roll each breast up carefully, wind a piece of cotton around to hold it, and dust with flour.

Heat 25 g/1 oz/2 tablespoons of the butter and the oil in a sauté pan and fry the chicken rolls over very low heat, turning frequently, until tender and golden, about 15 minutes. Remove the cotton, transfer the rolls to a hot serving dish and keep warm.

Add the Marsala, stock and remaining butter to the juices in the pan, bring to the boil and simmer for 3 to 4 minutes, while scraping up the juices from the base of the pan. Spoon over the rolls and garnish the dish with asparagus spears.
SERVES 4

# OSSOBUCO

*Braised Shin of Veal*

Each portion of ossobuco should be cut 5 cm/2 inches thick across a leg of veal so that each piece consists of the bone complete with the marrow in the centre, surrounded by meat. As suitable veal is not always readily available, it is wise to order it in advance.

**Metric/Imperial**
4 ossobuco, each weighing about 275 g/10 oz (see above)
flour for dusting
3 × 15 ml spoons/3 tablespoons olive oil
1 small onion, chopped
1 small carrot, chopped
1 stick celery, chopped
1 bay leaf
150 ml/¼ pint dry white wine
1 × 400 g/14 oz can peeled tomatoes
1 × 15 ml spoon/1 tablespoon tomato purée
salt
freshly ground black pepper
GREMOLATA:
1 clove garlic, chopped
grated rind of ½ lemon
2 × 15 ml spoons/2 tablespoons chopped fresh parsley

**American**
4 ossobuco, each weighing about 10 oz (see above)
flour for dusting
3 tablespoons olive oil
1 small onion, chopped
1 small carrot, chopped
1 stalk celery, chopped
1 bay leaf
⅔ cup dry white wine
1 × 14 oz can peeled tomatoes
1 tablespoon tomato paste
salt
freshly ground black pepper
GREMOLATA:
1 clove garlic, chopped
grated rind of ½ lemon
2 tablespoons chopped fresh parsley

Coat the pieces of meat with flour, handling carefully to avoid dislodging the marrow from the bones. Heat the oil in a large flameproof casserole and fry the meat quickly to seal and brown on both sides. Transfer to a plate.

Add the onion, carrot, celery and bay leaf to the pan, lower the heat and fry gently for 5 minutes, stirring occasionally. Add the wine and allow to bubble briskly until reduced by half. Add the tomatoes and their juice, the tomato purée (paste) and salt and pepper to taste. Bring to the boil, replace the meat, cover tightly and simmer gently for 1½ hours until tender.

Lift out the meat, arrange in a serving dish and keep hot. Purée the vegetables with the gravy in an electric blender or pass through a sieve and, if necessary, boil briskly until reduced to a medium thick sauce. Check the seasoning and pour over the meat.

Mix the ingredients of the *gremolata* together and sprinkle over the meat just before serving.

Traditionally, *ossobuco* is always accompanied by *Risotto alla Milanese* (see page 82) but no other vegetables.
SERVES 4

*Involtini di Petti di Pollo*

# VITELLO TONNATO

## Veal with Tuna Fish Mayonnaise

An unusual but delicious combination of cold veal with tuna fish mayonnaise. Make it the day before required so that the flavours have time to blend. Tuna fish mayonnaise is equally good for coating hard-boiled (hard-cooked) eggs.

### Metric/Imperial

1.25 kg/2½ lb piece boned roasting veal, preferably leg or loin
1 × 15 ml spoon/1 tablespoon oil
25 g/1 oz butter
salt
freshly ground black pepper
TUNA FISH MAYONNAISE:
1 × 90 g/3½ oz can tuna fish in oil
4 anchovy fillets
2 egg yolks
juice of ½ lemon
200 ml/⅓ pint olive oil
salt
white pepper
TO GARNISH:
anchovy fillets
capers, drained
lemon quarters
parsley sprigs

### American

2½ lb piece boned roasting veal, preferably leg or loin
1 tablespoon oil
2 tablespoons butter
salt
freshly ground black pepper
TUNA FISH MAYONNAISE:
1 × 3½ oz can tuna fish in oil
4 anchovy fillets
2 egg yolks
juice of ½ lemon
1 cup olive oil
salt
white pepper
TO GARNISH:
anchovy fillets
capers, drained
lemon quarters
parsley sprigs

Tie the veal into a neat roll.

Heat the oil and butter in a flameproof casserole and brown the veal lightly all over. Season with salt and pepper and cover the pan tightly. Transfer to the centre of a preheated moderate oven (160°C/325°F, Gas Mark 3) and cook for 1½ hours, basting once or twice. Leave to cool.

Meanwhile, make the tuna fish mayonnaise. Put the tuna fish with its oil, the anchovy fillets, egg yolks and 1 × 15 ml spoon/1 tablespoon of the lemon juice into a blender goblet and reduce to a purée. Blend in the oil, adding it very gradually at first, until the sauce thickens like a mayonnaise.

Alternatively, press the undrained tuna fish and the anchovy fillets through a sieve into a bowl, then whisk in the egg yolks. Whisking continuously, add the oil drop by drop. As the sauce thickens the oil may be added in a thin stream. Finally whisk in 1 × 15 ml spoon/1 tablespoon of the lemon juice.

Slice the cold veal fairly thinly and arrange in overlapping slices on a large serving platter. Thin the sauce to a coating consistency with either the remaining lemon juice or some of the veal juices, and spoon over the veal to cover it completely. Cover the dish loosely with foil and refrigerate overnight.

Before serving, garnish the dish with anchovy fillets, capers, lemon quarters and parsley. (Illustrated on page 2.)

SERVES 6 TO 8

Ossobuco with Risotto alla Milanese

Lombardy

# TACCHINO RIPIENO ARROSTO

*Stuffed Roast Turkey*

**Metric/Imperial**
4.5 kg/10 lb oven-ready turkey
salt
freshly ground black pepper
STUFFING:
0.5 kg/1 lb chestnuts
40 g/1½ oz butter
2 rashers streaky bacon, derinded and chopped
175 g/6 oz pork sausage meat
8 large prunes, soaked overnight, stoned and chopped
2 ripe pears, peeled and chopped
2 × 15 ml spoons/2 tablespoons brandy or dry white vermouth
salt
freshly ground black pepper
melted butter for basting

**American**
10 lb oven-ready turkey
salt
freshly ground black pepper
STUFFING:
1 lb chestnuts
3 tablespoons butter
2 bacon slices, derinded and chopped
¾ cup pork sausage meat
8 large prunes, soaked overnight, pitted and chopped
2 ripe pears, peeled and chopped
2 tablespoons brandy or dry white vermouth
salt
freshly ground black pepper
melted butter for basting

Remove the giblets from the turkey. Chop the liver and reserve. Wash and dry the turkey and season inside and out with salt and pepper.

To make the stuffing, cut a cross on the pointed end of each chestnut. Place the chestnuts in a pan, cover with water and simmer for 15 minutes. Drain, and while still hot peel off the shells and inner skins. Chop the chestnuts roughly. Melt the butter in a saucepan, fry the bacon for 1 to 2 minutes, then stir in the liver, chestnuts, sausage meat, prunes, pears, brandy or vermouth and salt and pepper to taste. Cool, then stuff loosely into the neck end of the turkey, putting any remaining stuffing into the body cavity.

Stand the turkey on a rack in a roasting tin, brush all over with melted butter and cover loosely with foil. Roast in the centre of a preheated moderate oven (180°C/

350°F, Gas Mark 4) for 1 hour. Lower the temperature to 160°C/325°F, Gas Mark 3 and cook for a further 2¼ to 3 hours, removing the foil for the last 30 minutes of cooking time. Transfer to a carving dish and trim with parsley, if liked.
SERVES 12 TO 15

Tacchino Ripieno Arrosto, Crema di Mascherpone with Pinoccate (page 61)

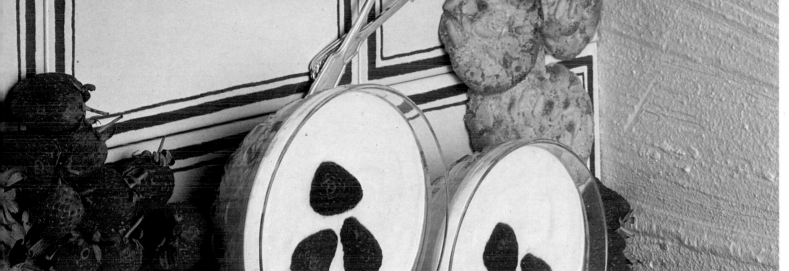

# SALSICCE CON VERZADA

*Sausages with Cabbage*

Although best made with rather spicy Italian pork sausages, any good pure pork sausages can be used.

**Metric/Imperial**
1 kg/2 lb firm white cabbage
50 g/2 oz butter
3 thin rashers streaky bacon, diced
1 medium onion, coarsely grated
2–3 × 15 ml spoons/2–3 tablespoons wine vinegar
salt
freshly ground black pepper
8 large pork sausages
2 × 15 ml spoons/2 tablespoons chopped fresh parsley

**American**
2 lb firm white cabbage
¼ cup butter
3 thin bacon slices, diced
1 medium onion, coarsely grated
2–3 tablespoons wine vinegar
salt
freshly ground black pepper
8 large pork sausages
2 tablespoons chopped fresh parsley

Remove any discoloured outer leaves from the cabbage. Cut into quarters, discard the hard core and wash in cold salted water. Drain, and shred finely.

Melt the butter in a large heavy pan and fry the bacon and onion very gently for 5 minutes. Add the cabbage and stir until coated with butter. Cover the pan and cook over moderate heat until the cabbage begins to soften. Add the vinegar and salt and pepper to taste and stir well.

Prick the sausages with a fork and lay on top of the cabbage. Cover tightly and cook over low heat for about 1 hour, checking from time to time that the cabbage is not sticking to the pan. Alternatively, cook in a preheated moderate oven (160°C/325°F, Gas Mark 3) for about 1 hour.

Place the cabbage in a shallow dish, arrange the sausages on top and sprinkle with parsley.
SERVES 4

# CREMA DI MASCHERPONE

*Cream Cheese Dessert*

Mascherpone is a butter-yellow soft cream cheese made in Lombardy. Any fresh soft cream cheese can be used instead.

**Metric/Imperial**
225 g/8 oz soft cream cheese
2 eggs, separated
50 g/2 oz caster sugar
2 × 15 ml spoons/2 tablespoons orange liqueur, brandy or rum
225 g/8 oz fresh raspberries or small strawberries

**American**
1 cup soft cream cheese
2 eggs, separated
¼ cup sugar
2 tablespoons orange liqueur, brandy, or rum
1½ cups fresh raspberries or small strawberries

Press the cream cheese through a sieve (strainer) into a mixing bowl. Beat in the egg yolks and sugar and then the liqueur or spirit, beating until the mixture is light. Whisk the egg whites until firm but not stiff, and fold lightly but thoroughly into the cream.

Pile the mixture into a large serving dish, or individual dishes and top with raspberries or strawberries. Serve with crisp biscuits such as *pinoccate* (see page 61).
SERVES 4

# MONTE BIANCO

*Chestnut Purée with Cream*

There are many versions of this dessert, ranging from elaborate restaurant confections to this simple recipe which seems to resemble the snow-capped Mont Blanc better than most. Serve soon after preparing this dish.

**Metric/Imperial**
0.5 kg/1 lb chestnuts
175 g/6 oz icing sugar, sifted
pinch of salt
2 × 15 ml spoons/2 tablespoons brandy, rum or Strega
150 ml/¼ pint double cream

**American**
1 lb chestnuts
1¼ cups confectioners' sugar, sifted
pinch of salt
2 tablespoons brandy, rum or Strega
⅔ cup heavy cream

Using a sharp knife, cut a cross at the pointed end of each chestnut. Put them in a pan, cover with water, bring to the boil and simmer for 15 minutes. Drain, and while still hot peel off the shells and inner skins.

Cover the chestnuts with cold water and simmer for 45 minutes or until they are very soft. Strain off the water, leaving the chestnuts in the pan. Mash them smoothly, then beat in the sugar and salt. Pile the chestnut purée into a mound on a serving dish.

Add the brandy, rum or liqueur to the cream and whip until thick but not stiff. Swirl it lightly over the top of the mound, leaving the base uncovered.

Alternatively, spoon the chestnut purée into individual glass dishes and swirl the cream on top (as shown on page 2).
SERVES 4

# Piemonte

Occupying the North-West corner of Italy and enjoying a long, mountainous border with France, Piemonte is a region of contrasts. Overlooked by Mont Blanc and the Matterhorn, much of the country is mountainous, as the name Piemonte (at the foot of the mountains) suggests. The lower slopes of the Alps give way to forests, and the region is trellised with fast-flowing streams which feed the great river Po as it makes its majestic way across Northern Italy to the Adriatic. This varied terrain gives Piemonte a rich variety of local food products. The native inhabitants of Piemonte are a mixture of mountain folk and aristocratic families, and the gastronomic traditions reflect a sophisticated cuisine combined with a more robust rustic fare.

The river valleys are exceedingly fertile and produce excellent vegetables such as asparagus, celery, peppers, artichokes and onions, and in spite of the northern latitude, grapes, peaches and strawberries flourish. In the province of Novara, the streams are diverted to create paddy fields which have made Piemonte the rice bowl of Italy.

Cheese is produced in quantity, the most renowned being Fontina, a rich, creamy cheese made from the milk of selected breeds of cattle, originally a product of the Valle d'Aosta. Fontina melts creamily and is featured in several regional recipes.

The forest areas in the north of the region support game such as wild boar, chamois, goat and hare, and these are cooked in strongly flavoured sauces, but you are only likely to find these dishes in the mountains where the animals are caught. Game birds like pheasant and partridge are more plentiful. Probably the most highly prized product of the area is the white truffle. These 'diamonds of the table' are found largely in the forest area south of Alba.

In the cold mountain areas, the food becomes very substantial and thick vegetable soups, boiled meats and highly seasoned garlic-flavoured dishes are popular. A dish which reflects the traditional method of cooking over a fire is *bolliti misti* (mixed boiled meats). Provided you have a large enough pot, a family gathering can be catered for in one huge cooking utensil, into which go a variety of different meats: beef, tongue, sausage, chicken and veal, and vegetables. Turin, the great industrial capital of Piemonte, is famous for the invention of *grissini* (breadsticks) made from locally grown wheat and for vermouth, a white aperitif made from local white wine blended with spirits, herbs and bitters. Dry white vermouth is useful as a substitute for white wine in recipes and is particularly good in fish, chicken and veal dishes.

Last but by no means least Piemonte is the greatest wine producing region of Italy. The south-facing lower slopes of the mountains grow the grapes which produce such excellent red table wines as barolo, barbaresco and gattinara to accompany roasts and grills, as well as the dark barbera to accompany the more robust and highly seasoned dishes. This region also produces some well known white wines, including the semi-sweet sparkling asti spumante.

# BAGNO CALDO

*Garlic and Anchovy Hot Dip*

This is one of the very robust traditional dishes of Piemonte, for which you need a strong digestion.

There are many exciting variations of the recipe, but always in Piemonte the dip is kept hot over a spirit stove in the centre of the table and surrounded with sticks of crisp, raw vegetables for dipping. Cardoons, a type of edible thistle, are popular locally for dipping, but any crisp vegetable is suitable. *Grissini* (bread sticks) are served at the same time and this hearty meal starter or snack is swilled down with coarse red wine.

**Metric/Imperial**

ACCOMPANIMENTS:

2 carrots
2 sticks celery
1 bulb fennel
1 red pepper, halved and seeded
1 green pepper, halved and seeded
few spring onions
100 g/4 oz button mushrooms

DIP:

6 cloves garlic, crushed
6 anchovy fillets, mashed
6 × 15 ml spoons/6 tablespoons olive oil
75 g/3 oz butter
1 small white truffle, thinly sliced (if available)

**American**

ACCOMPANIMENTS:

2 carrots
2 stalks celery
1 bulb fennel
1 red pepper, halved and seeded
1 green pepper, halved and seeded
few scallions
¼ lb button mushrooms

DIP:

6 cloves garlic, crushed
6 anchovy fillets, mashed
6 tablespoons olive oil
6 tablespoons butter
1 small white truffle, thinly sliced (if available)

Prepare the vegetables and divide into strips or pieces roughly 1 × 5 cm/½ × 2 inches. Leave the mushrooms whole, or cut in quarters if large.

To prepare the dip, pound the garlic and anchovy fillets to a paste then gradually stir in the oil. Put into a small pan with the butter and leave over a low heat for about 10 minutes, stirring occasionally. Transfer the pan to a spirit stove if available, and surround with vegetables and bread sticks.

Add the white truffle, if using, just before serving.

SERVES 4

# PEPERONI ALLA PIEMONTESE

*Peppers stuffed with Tomatoes, Anchovies and Garlic*

These stuffed peppers make a splendidly colourful platter for a summer buffet and are much enjoyed by garlic and anchovy addicts. Choose round, even-sized peppers.

**Metric/Imperial**

4 green peppers
4 yellow peppers
8 large tomatoes, skinned and quartered
8 anchovy filets
4 cloves garlic, crushed
8 × 15 ml spoons/8 tablespoons olive oil

**American**

4 green peppers
4 yellow peppers
8 large tomatoes, skinned and quartered
8 anchovy filets
4 cloves garlic, crushed
½ cup olive oil

Cut the peppers lengthwise in half and discard the pith and seeds. Wash and drain the peppers and arrange side by side, hollow sides up, in an oiled, shallow ovenproof dish.

Put two tomato quarters into each pepper half. Mash the anchovy fillets with a fork, add the garlic and oil and mix thoroughly. Put a little of this mixture into each pepper.

Cook, uncovered, in a preheated moderate oven (180°C/350°F, Gas Mark 4) for 30 to 35 minutes. Take care not to overcook as the peppers should retain a little of their crispness. Serve cold as an antipasto or as part of a buffet.

SERVES 6 TO 8

# FONDUTA

*Fondue*

Fonduta is not unlike a Swiss fondue, but is different in flavour because an authentic fonduta can only be made from Fontina, a rich and creamy Piemonte cheese originating in the valley of Aosta. The cheese comes in large wheel shapes and is generally available in Italian delicatessen stores.

Serve *Fonduta* as an unusual hors d'oeuvres for a dinner party or as a colourful buffet party dish.

**Metric/Imperial**

175 g/6 oz Fontina cheese
milk for soaking
2 egg yolks, lightly beaten
15 g/½ oz butter
salt
freshly ground white pepper
grated nutmeg (optional)

GARNISH:

few thin slices of white bread, cut into small triangles and toasted
1 small white truffle, very thinly sliced (optional)

**American**

6 oz Fontina cheese
milk for soaking
2 egg yolks, lightly beaten
1 tablespoon butter
salt
freshly ground white pepper
grated nutmeg (optional)

GARNISH:

few thin slices of white bread, cut into small triangles and toasted
1 small white truffle, very thinly sliced (optional)

## Bagno Caldo, Fondura

Trim off any rind and slice the cheese into small, thin pieces. Put into a basin, cover with milk and leave to soak for 4 to 6 hours. Drain the cheese, reserving the milk, and put the cheese into the top of a double saucepan or into a bowl over a saucepan of hot water. Add 2 × 15 ml spoons/2 tablespoons of the milk, the egg yolks, butter, and seasoning and nutmeg to taste.

Cook over gently simmering water, stirring frequently, until the ingredients melt into a thick, smooth cream. Pour immediately into individual soup bowls and stand triangles of toast around the edge. If using the truffle, sprinkle the slices over the surface and serve at once.

SERVES 2

---

*Green Sauce*

# SALSA VERDE

This refreshing, slightly sharp sauce is traditionally served with *bollito* (see page 92), but is equally delicious with cold meats and even better with cold fish. A few chopped anchovy fillets are sometimes included in the recipe.

**Metric/Imperial**
50 g/2 oz fresh parsley leaves
1 shallot
1 clove garlic
1 × 15 ml spoon/1 tablespoon drained capers
4 × 15 ml spoons/4 tablespoons olive oil
salt
freshly ground black pepper

**American**
2 oz fresh parsley leaves
1 shallot
1 clove garlic
1 tablespoon drained capers
¼ cup olive oil
juice of 1 lemon
salt
freshly ground black pepper

Chop the parsley, shallot, garlic and capers very finely. Put into a basin and stir in the oil, lemon juice and seasoning to taste. Alternatively, if you have an electric blender, simply put all the ingredients into the goblet and blend for about 1 minute until the parsley and shallot are finely chopped and the sauce is evenly mixed.

MAKES ABOUT 150 ML/¼ PINT/⅔ CUP SAUCE

# TROTINE AI FUNGHI

*Trout with Mushrooms*

The lakes and streams of Piemonte abound with trout, and in this recipe they are attractively combined with sliced mushrooms and crisp breadcrumbs.

**Metric/Imperial**
350 g/12 oz button mushrooms
4 trout, each about 275 g/10 oz
salt
freshly ground black pepper
flour for coating
1 tablespoon oil
6 tablespoons butter
2 spring onions, finely sliced
1 tablespoon chopped fresh parsley
juice of ½ lemon
25 g/1 oz dry white breadcrumbs
GARNISH:
lemon quarters
sprigs of parsley

**American**
3 cups button mushrooms
4 trout, each about 10 oz
salt
freshly ground black pepper
flour for coating
1 tablespoon oil
6 tablespoons butter
2 scallions, finely sliced
1 tablespoon chopped fresh parsley
juice of ½ lemon
½ cup dry white bread crumbs
GARNISH:
lemon quarters
sprigs of parsley

Wash but do not peel the mushrooms, then cut into thin slices. Wash the trout, leaving the heads and tails on, and pat dry. Season inside and out with salt and pepper and then coat lightly with flour. Heat the oil and 25 g/1 oz/2 tablespoons of the butter in a large frying pan (skillet) and fry the trout gently for 6 to 8 minutes on each side, until lightly browned.

In another pan, melt 40 g/1½ oz/3 tablespoons butter and fry the spring onions (scallions) and mushrooms fairly briskly until the mushrooms begin to soften, about 3 to 5 minutes. Add 1 × 2.5 ml spoon/½ teaspoon salt, the parsley and lemon juice and toss lightly.

Arrange the trout side by side on a large hot dish with rows of mushrooms in between them. Keep hot. Quickly fry the breadcrumbs in the pan in which the fish were cooked, adding more butter if necessary, and when crisp sprinkle over fish. Garnish with lemon and parsley.
SERVES 4

# FILETTI DI TACCHINO ALLA PIEMONTESE

*Turkey Breasts with Marsala*

This recipe has been adapted to use mushrooms instead of the white truffles which, even in Piemonte, are only available during the winter.

**Metric/Imperial**
0.5 kg/1 lb boneless turkey breast meat, skin removed
salt
freshly ground black pepper
flour for coating
65 g/2½ oz butter
1 × 15 ml spoon/1 tablespoon oil
100 g/4 oz button mushrooms, thinly sliced
2 × 15 ml spoons/2 tablespoons grated Parmesan cheese
6 × 15 ml spoons/6 tablespoons Marsala
2 × 15 ml spoons/2 tablespoons turkey or chicken stock
GARNISH:
cooked broccoli or asparagus spears
lemon wedges

**American**
1 lb boneless turkey breast meat, skin removed
salt
freshly ground black pepper
flour for coating
5 tablespoons butter
1 tablespoon oil
1 cup thinly sliced button mushrooms
2 tablespoons grated Parmesan cheese
6 tablespoons Marsala
2 tablespoons turkey or chicken stock
GARNISH:
cooked broccoli or asparagus spears
lemon wedges

Cut the turkey breast meat into 5 mm/¼ inch thick slices to make 4 portions. Place the slices between damp greaseproof (waxed) paper and flatten a little with a rolling pin. Dust the turkey slices with salt, pepper and flour. Heat 25 g/1 oz/2 tablespoons butter and the oil in a heavy frying pan (skillet) and fry the turkey slices very gently for 15 minutes, or until tender. Transfer to a shallow flameproof dish and keep warm.

Melt another 25 g/1 oz/2 tablespoons butter in the pan, and fry the mushrooms for 2 to 3 minutes, stirring frequently. Remove from the pan with a slotted spoon, spread over the turkey slices and sprinkle with the Parmesan cheese.

Pour the Marsala and the turkey or chicken stock into the frying pan (skillet) and boil rapidly, stirring up the juices from the base of the pan, until reduced by half. Stir in the remaining butter and spoon the sauce over the turkey and mushrooms. Place under a preheated grill (broiler) for 1 to 2 minutes until the cheese melts.

Serve immediately garnished with asparagus or broccoli spears and lemon wedges.
SERVES 4

# BOLLITO MISTO

*Mixed Boiled Meats*

The Bollito originated in the country districts of Piemonte in the days when cooking was done over an open fire. A selection of boiling meats are cooked together in one huge pot, so it is a dish for large gatherings only. The principle of Bollito is simple. The meat requiring the longest cooking time is started first and the others are added to the pot according to the time they need. The recipe below is typical, but other boiling meats such as calf's head or pig's feet can be added, or even a capon or small turkey.

**Metric/Imperial**
1 small ox tongue, lightly salted
1–1.5 kg/2–3 lb boned and rolled joint of veal or beef
2 onions, quartered
2 carrots, quartered
2 sticks celery, sliced
salt
10 peppercorns
2 bay leaves
1–1.5 kg/2–3 lb oven-ready chicken
1 cotechino (Italian pork sausage) (see page 91)
salsa verde (see page 91)

**American**
1 small ox tongue, lightly salted
2–3 lb boned and rolled cut of veal or beef for roasting
2 onions, quartered
2 carrots, quartered
2 stalks celery, sliced
salt
10 peppercorns
2 bay leaves
2–3 lb oven-ready chicken
1 cotechino (Italian pork sausage)
salsa verde (see page 91)

Put the tongue into a deep pan, cover with cold water, bring slowly to the boil, then drain. Add fresh water to cover and simmer very gently for 1 hour. Skim. Add the veal or beef, onions, carrots, celery, salt, peppercorns and bay leaves and add sufficient water just to cover the meat. Bring to the boil, skim, and continue simmering for another 1½ hours. Add the chicken and the cotechino, well pricked to prevent the skin bursting. Cover and simmer for a further 1 hour or until all the meats are tender.

Lift out the meats, arrange on large dishes and carve as required. Serve the meat with a little of the broth poured over to moisten it. (The rest of the broth makes an excellent base for soups.)

Serve the *bollito* with boiled haricot (navy) beans, cabbage and potatoes and hand around a large bowl of *salsa verde*.

SERVES 16 TO 20

# MANZO BRASATO AL VINO ROSSO

*Beef Braised in Red Wine*

An excellent way of cooking a joint of braising beef in a robust Piemonte wine. Barolo is often quoted as 'the' wine to use, but one of the lesser and cheaper red wines will do admirably, provided it is full bodied.

**Metric/Imperial**
1.5 kg/3 lb joint of topside, chuck or rolled brisket
2 onions
1 carrot
1 stick celery, sliced
2 cloves garlic
2 bay leaves
6 peppercorns
½ bottle red wine
25 g/1 oz bacon fat or dripping
salt
*freshly ground black pepper*

**American**
3 lb top round, chuck roast or rolled brisket
2 onions
1 carrot
1 stalk celery, sliced
2 cloves garlic
2 bay leaves
6 peppercorns
½ bottle red wine
2 tablespoons fatback or dripping
salt
*freshly ground black pepper*

Put the meat into a deep basin. Slice one of the onions and chop the other one very finely. Add the sliced onion, carrot, celery, garlic, bay leaves, peppercorns and wine to the meat. Cover and leave to marinate for 24 hours, turning several times.

Lift the meat out of the marinade and

dry it carefully. Heat the fat in a flame-proof casserole into which the meat will fit fairly closely. Add the chopped onion to the casserole and fry gently for about 5 minutes. Put in the meat, increase the heat and brown the meat on all sides. Pour in the strained marinade and bring to the boil. Season with salt and pepper, lower the heat so that the casserole barely simmers, cover tightly and simmer very gently for at least 3 hours or until the meat is tender, turning the meat once half-way through. Transfer meat to a carving dish.

At the end of the cooking there should be just enough sauce to moisten each portion. If there is too much, reduce the sauce by rapid boiling. On the other hand should the liquid evaporate too quickly during cooking, add a little stock or water.

Slice the meat fairly thickly and arrange in a hot serving dish. Skim any surface fat from the sauce, check the seasoning and spoon over the meat. Serve with buttered ribbon pasta or *gnocchi*.

SERVES 6

Trotine ai Funghi, Manzo Brasato al Vino Rosso

*Piemonte*

# PESCHE RIPIENE

*Stuffed Baked Peaches*

**Metric/Imperial**
4 large, firm ripe peaches
50 g/2 oz fine sponge cake crumbs
50 g/2 oz ground almonds or hazelnuts
50 g/2 oz caster sugar
25 g/1 oz butter, softened
juice of 1 lemon

**American**
4 large, firm ripe peaches
1 cup fine sponge cake crumbs
½ cup ground almonds or filberts
¼ cup sugar
2 tablespoons butter, softened
juice of 1 lemon

Immerse the peaches in boiling water for a few seconds to loosen the skins, then drain and plunge into cold water. Peel, halve and remove the stones (seeds). Using a teaspoon, scoop enough flesh from each half to make a deep indentation for the stuffing. Chop the peach flesh.

Mix the peach flesh with the cake crumbs, nuts, sugar, butter and lemon juice to moisten. Pile the stuffing into the peach halves and smooth the top.

Arrange the peaches side by side in a shallow, well buttered ovenproof dish. Bake in a preheated moderate oven (180°C/350°F, Gas Mark 4) for 30 to 35 minutes. Serve hot, warm or cold.
SERVES 4

# ZUPPA DI CILIEGE

*Cherries in Red Wine*

Another recipe using the good red wine of Piemonte.

**Metric/Imperial**
100 g/4 oz sugar
1 thin strip of orange rind, zest only
pinch of powdered cinnamon
1 × 15 ml spoon/1 tablespoon
  redcurrant jelly
150 ml/¼ pint red wine
0.5 kg/1 lb large black cherries, stoned
butter for shallow frying
4 thin small slices of bread, crusts
  removed

**American**
½ cup sugar
1 thin strip of orange rind, zest only
pinch of powdered cinnamon
1 tablespoon redcurrant jelly
⅔ cup red wine
1 lb large bing cherries, pitted
butter for shallow frying
4 thin small slices of bread, crusts
  removed

Put the sugar, orange rind, cinnamon, redcurrant jelly and wine into a saucepan. Heat gently until the sugar has dissolved then boil for 1 minute. Add the cherries and simmer gently for 10 to 15 minutes.

Melt the butter in a large frying pan (skillet) and fry the bread slices until golden each side. Drain and arrange in 4 shallow plates. Using a perforated spoon, drain the cherries and arrange on the bread slices.

Reduce the syrup by boiling rapidly for a few minutes, then strain over the cherries and serve hot.
SERVES 4

Zuppa di Ciliege, Pesche Ripiene

# ITALIAN RESTAURANTS AROUND THE WORLD

## GREAT BRITAIN & IRELAND

GENNARO'S   44 Dean St., LONDON W1
LA BUSSOLA   42 St. Martin's Lane, LONDON WC2
LEONIS QUO VADIS   26–29 Dean St., LONDON WC2
TIBERIO   22 Queen St., LONDON W1
VILLA DEI CESARI   135 Grosvenor Rd., LONDON SW1
LA CAPPANA   Hurst Rd., BIRMINGHAM
SARACENO   15 Magdalen St., OXFORD
TERRAZZA   Minerva House, 16 Greek St., LEEDS
TERRAZZA   14 Nicholas St., MANCHESTER
COSMO   58 North Castle St., Edinburgh, SCOTLAND
LA CAPANNINA   65–67 Halket Place, St. Helier, JERSEY
GINO'S   Market Square, Cork St., S. IRELAND

## U.S.A.

ORSINI'S   41 West 56th St., NEW YORK
ROMEO SALTA   39 West 56th St., NEW YORK
SAN MARINO   236 East 53rd St., NEW YORK
LA SCALA   9455 Santa Monica Boulevard, NEW YORK
STEFANINO'S TRATTORIA   9229 Sunset Boulevard,
FLORIDA   Holywood, FLORIDA
CASA SANTINO   12155 Biscayne Boulevard, Miami,
FLORIDA
PICCIOLO   2nd St., Collins Ave., Miami Beach, FLORIDA
GUSTI'S   1837 M. St., N. W. WASHINGTON D.C.
ROMA   3419 Connecticut Ave., N. W. WASHINGTON D.C.

## AUSTRALIA

SORRENTO   135 Hindley St., Adelaide, SOUTH AUSTRALIA
MILANO   78 Queen St., Brisbane, QUEENSLAND
FLORENTINO   80 Bourke St., Melbourne, VICTORIA
ARRIVEDERCI   77 William St., Kings Cross, Sydney,
NEW SOUTH WALES
BEPPI'S   Yurong St., NEW SOUTH WALES
LA ZAGARA   132 Norton St., Sydney, NEW SOUTH WALES

## ITALY

EL TOULÀ   via della Lupa 29, ROMA
SANS SOUCI   via Sicilia 20/24, ROMA
GIANNINO   via Amorre Sciesa 8, MILANO
FINI   largo San Francesco, MODENA
CHARLESTON   via della Libertà 37, Palermo, SICILY
AL GATTO NERO   corso Filippo Turati 14, TORINO
ANTICO MARTINI   campo San Fantin 1983, VENEZIA
12 APOSTOLI   corticella San Marco 3, VERONA

## AUSTRIA

GROTTA AZZURA   1 Babenbergerstrasse 5, VIENNA
RISTORANTE DA LUCIANO   VII Sigmundsgasse 14,
VIENNA
ZUM GRUNEN ANKER   1 Grünangergasse 10, VIENNA
CAMINO   Riedenburgerstrasse 2, SALZBURG

## SWITZERLAND

DA ROBERTO   Kuechengasse 3, 4000 BASEL
RISTORANTE GIARDINO   6614 BRISSAGO
RESTAURANT DU CHEVAL-BLANC   1253
Vandoeuvres, GENEVA
BOLOGNESE   Stampfenbachstrasse 38, 8000 ZURICH
CASA FERLIN   Kasernenstrasse 75, 8000 ZURICH
DE BONI   Lagerstrasse 121, 8000 ZURICH

## FRANCE

CHEZ JEAN FRANCO   9 rue Racine, 75006 PARIS
SAN FRANCISCO   64 Avenue de Versailles, 75005 PARIS
IL TEATRO   38 rue de Buci, 75006 PARIS
POLPETTA   2 rue Paradis, MONTE-CARLO
DON CAMILLO   5 rue Ponchettes, NICE

## GERMANY

DA BRUNO   Elbestrasse 15, FRANKFURT
ENNIO'S RISTORANTE   An der Alster 23, HAMBURG
SANTA LUCIA   Badenwerkstrasse 1, KARLSRUHE
RISTORANTE ALFREDO   Turisstrasse, KÖLN
EL TOULÀ   Sparkassenstrasse 5, MÜNCHEN
IL SORRISO   Kurfurstenstrasse, WEST BERLIN

## BELGIUM

FRANCESCO   23 Rue Jourdan, 1060 BRUXELLES
MEO PATACCA   20 Rue Jourdan, 1060 BRUXELLES
VILLA BORGHESE   24 Rue Dejoncker, 1060 BRUXELLES
BOCCALINO & DANY'S   2 Avenue Brassine, 1640
RHODE ST-GENÈSE

## THE NETHERLANDS

ISOLA BELLA   Thorbeckeplein 7–9, 1017 CS AMSTERDAM
PORTO ERCOLE   Leidsekruisstraat 11, 1017 RE
AMSTERDAM
LA GONDOLA   Noordeinde 196, THE HAGUE
IL VESUVIO   Laan van Meedervoort 14, THE HAGUE

## DENMARK

LA GUITARRA   21 Fiolstraede, COPENHAGEN
RISTORANTE ITALIANO   2 Fiolstraede, COPENHAGEN
STEPHAN A PORTA   17 Kongens Nytory, COPENHAGEN

## NORWAY

BELLA NAPOLI   Storgt. 26, OSLO 1
LA POPINA   Haakon VII gt. 5, OSLO 1
VALENTES OSTERIA ITALIANA   Kirkeveien, OSLO 3

## SWEDEN

IL POZZO   Skeppargatan 16, STOCKHOLM
RODOLFO   Storkyrkobrinken 16, STOCKHOLM
LA SCALA RISTORANTE   Götaplatsen, GOTHENBURG
PAPAGALLO   Första Långatan 8, GOTHENBURG

# ACKNOWLEDGMENTS

All photography by Bob Golden except for:
J. Allan Cash 26–27, 78–79, 88–89; Angel Studio 20; Rex
Bamber 71; Melvin Grey 34 above left, 40, 60; Sonia Halliday
54–55; Paf International 46; Pentangle Photography 38; Zefa
(G. Barone) 62–63, (Studio Benser) 18–19, (W. F. Davidson)
70–71, (R. Everts) 36–37, (Starfoto) 44–45.

The publishers would like to thank the following companies
for the loan of accessories for photography:
Britannia Catering Equipment Ltd; British Crafts Centre;
Casa Pupo; Craftsmen Potters' Association; Elizabeth David Ltd;
Elon Tiles Ltd; D. H. Evans; Jaeggi Leon & Sons Ltd; Sally
Lawford's Country Kitchen; Harvey Nichols & Co Ltd.